TWICE HAVE THE
TRUMPETS SOUNDED

Twice have the trumpets sounded;
The generous and gravest citizens
Have hent the gates . . .

MEASURE FOR MEASURE, IV.6

OEDIPUS AND THE CHORUS

TWICE HAVE THE TRUMPETS SOUNDED

*A Record of
the Stratford Shakespearean Festival
in Canada
1954*

TYRONE GUTHRIE
ROBERTSON DAVIES
GRANT MACDONALD

CLARKE, IRWIN & COMPANY LIMITED, TORONTO

Printed in Canada

CONTENTS

ILLUSTRATIONS

Measure for Measure

Oedipus Rex

viii

PREFACE

BECAUSE OF the friendly reception which was given to the record of the 1953 Shakespeare Festival at Stratford, Ontario, called *Renown at Stratford,* the collaborators who produced that book are encouraged to offer the public this volume about the 1954 season. It is not 'the mixture as before', but a book of different character. It contains comment on the future of the festival, by Dr. Tyrone Guthrie, a pictorial record of the plays by Grant Macdonald, and four essays, one on each of the productions and one on Dr. Guthrie's methods of rehearsal, by the present writer.

These essays are extended notices of the plays, but they are not precisely what I would have written if I had been preparing them for a daily paper—supposing that any paper could allow a critic the time or the space to write at such length. They are not first-night judgments (which critics and actors both deplore but cannot escape) because I have been able to take time to see the plays more than once, and have had some leisure in which to think about them. For these reasons I may have put emphasis on things which those who saw the plays will find surprising, and I may not have mentioned things which they thought worthy of censure. The newspaper critic may fitly complain of matters which can be put right in subsequent performances, to the betterment of the play. But what would be the purpose of such complaints here, when the festival is long over, and the tent put away till next

Spring? I have tried to write about what was durable in these productions, and what lingers in memory is almost entirely pleasant and calls for praise.

The writer offers this explanation, because some people said that what was written in *Renown at Stratford* was not critical enough. But what is criticism? Is it chiefly fault-finding? Who cares now if Mr. X was irritatingly uncertain of his lines at a particular performance, or if a pistol failed to explode on a certain night? Are these trivialities to be remembered now? My own view is that the critic should be of the temperament which a devout wit has ascribed to Almighty God—'easy to please, but hard to satisfy'. If I have been greatly pleased by most of what I saw at Stratford, is it to be assumed that I am satisfied with all of it? There is room, surely, for a critic who would rather praise than blame, when praise may honestly be tendered?

Nevertheless, there is some blame in these pages. There were English visitors to the 1953 festival, and some English readers of *Renown at Stratford*, who felt that too much fuss was being made about some Shakespearean performances which were rather remote from the hub of the universe. Canadians are familiar with the friendly desire of our English cousins to keep us from growing conceited. But I do not think that these kindly folk, so zealous for our spiritual well-being, understand the Canadian temperament, or know how far we are from self-satisfaction in anything relating to the arts; what might appear as dangerous conceit in an Englishman is often, in a Canadian, no more than the dawn of self-reliance. Only those who know how anxiously the beginnings of the Stratford Festival were watched, and how its success relieved a desperate tension, may say how much praise is permissible in writing about it. But, for those to whom blame is a necessary ingredient in any criticism, there is some blame here.

In the main, however, these are unashamed tributes to a venture of which Canada is proud, with a pride which is in no danger of becoming inordinate or self-destructive. We, who would have had to bury the corpse if the festival had failed, must not be considered naïve if we rejoice to see it in robust health.

Once again, it has been an unalloyed pleasure to work with Dr. Guthrie and Mr. Macdonald in the preparation of this book.

ROBERTSON DAVIES

October 1
1 9 5 4

ACKNOWLEDGMENTS

The pencil sketches of James Mason as Angelo, of Donald Harron as Tranio, of Lloyd Bochner as the Duke disguised, of Douglas Campbell as Baptista, and of Eleanor Stuart as herself have appeared in *The Sketch*. The artist wishes to express his thanks to the editors for permission to reproduce them here.

The quotations from W. B. Yeats' translation of 'Oedipus Rex' are from *Collected Plays of W. B. Yeats*, published by Macmillan & Company Limited, and have been used here with the permission of Mrs. Yeats and the publishers.

The quotations from Gilbert Murray's translation of *Oedipus: King of Thebes* have been used here with the permission of Messrs. Allen & Unwin.

THE STRATFORD SHAKESPEAREAN FESTIVAL OF CANADA FOUNDATION

Under the distinguished patronage of
His Excellency
Rt. Hon. Vincent Massey, C.H., P.C., LL.D., D.C.L.
Governor-General of Canada

OFFICERS

H. A. Showalter, Ph.D., President

A. M. Bell, Vice-President   Mrs. C. Elspeth Hall, Secretary

William H. Kalbfleisch, Treasurer

BOARD OF GOVERNORS

FOR THE STRATFORD SHAKESPEAREAN FESTIVAL OF CANADA FOUNDATION

ARTISTIC DIRECTOR	Cecil Clarke
DIRECTOR OF PLANNING	Tom Patterson
DIRECTOR OF ADMINISTRATION	Roy Loken
PRODUCTION MANAGER	Tom Brown

STAGE MANAGEMENT

STAGE DIRECTOR	Elspeth Cochrane
STAGE MANAGER	John Hayes
ASSISTANT STAGE MANAGERS	Jack Merigold
	Donal S. Wilson

REHEARSAL
A STUDY IN RHYTHM

By ROBERTSON DAVIES

REHEARSAL IS A WORD which comes to us from French, and its literal meaning is 'to harrow repeatedly'; and while we all know that 'to harrow' means to cultivate, it is not without significance in the present connection that its earlier meaning was 'to tear, lacerate or wound'. Many people are curious about rehearsals, but misconceptions of the nature of rehearsal are common even among experienced playgoers. Movies, in which rehearsal is presented as a Bedlam of disorganization, bad temper, improvisation and sudden inspiration, conducted by people in the last stages of frenzy, have done nothing to dispel these groundless ideas. The notion persists that the rehearsal of a play is less a matter of repeated harrowing than an orgy of tearing, laceration and wounding. Some description of the methods of Tyrone Guthrie, one of the master-rehearsers of our day, may correct this misplaced emphasis, and entertain those who are really anxious to know what means are used to prepare a play for public performance.

Before we can follow Dr. Guthrie to a rehearsal, however, we must have some clear idea of what his job will be when he gets there. The director of a play, in the modern theatre, is its principal interpreter. The actors, the designer, the composer of the music, all bring their abilities to the service of the finished production, but these abilities must be co-ordinated by the director, and given their appropriate place and emphasis in a plan which he has already formed. Long before rehearsals begin he has made his plan, and at the first rehearsal he will explain it, in broad outline, to everyone concerned.

3

It is certain that before rehearsals begin he will have had many talks with the designer, and the designs of costumes and properties will be ready for the whole company to see. This is important, for the finished articles may not be ready until a few days before the opening. Very probably, also, he will have discussed his approach to the play with the principal actors. Dr. Guthrie, who draws very well, likes to make sketches of costumes and make-up, some of which serve to give Miss Moiseiwitsch springboards for her own invention; others she may use very much as he draws them, but with the additional directions about cut, finish and materials without which the technicians cannot go to work. Dr. Guthrie also has determined ideas about music, and the musical accompaniments to his productions strongly reflect his own taste. He sings remarkably well, and plays the piano with spirit. Before rehearsals begin roughly half the work on a production has been done. It is not usual for such work to be continuous, and it may be taken up at intervals over a period of several months.

The director's most important task, of course, is to decide what his approach to the play will be, to form his opinion about it, and to choose the means which he will use to carry it out. Unless he is a beginner at his job, he brings to this task qualities of experience, understanding and a matured talent which are his principal stock-in-trade. The techniques and skills of the theatre can be, and are, acquired by scores of people who never gain this final, complex interpretative ability which makes a man a theatrical director of the first rank.

His intellectual equipment is strikingly similar to that of the conductor of an orchestra. The conductor has stored away in his brain the scores of a large number of major musical works; he knows them in the minutest detail; he knows what he can get out of a first-rate orchestra in the performance of a particular work, and he knows pretty shrewdly what he can get out of a strange orchestra, not of the first rank, if he has to conduct without adequate rehearsal. The theatrical director probably has the text of twenty plays of Shakespeare and a few other classical plays stored in his brain, and even if his own recitation of particular passages from them may not be word-perfect, his ear will note a fault when an actor makes one. He too can judge very quickly what he will be able to bring out of a particular company of actors.

This analogy must not be carried too far, however, for music permits of certainties which are impossible in the theatre. Musical audiences are willing and eager to hear a celebrated conductor's interpretation of a great work, in every important city in the world, and more than once. But the theatrical director cannot carry his ideas from country to country with so much success, and critics are quick to remark on it if he repeats his effects. However often he may have directed *The Taming of the Shrew*, for instance, he is expected to do it differently every time.

But the play is always the same. Unless he falsifies what the author has written, and distorts the emphasis which the author has indicated, how is the necessary novelty achieved? Plainly, by a faithful and respectful adherence to the essential truth of the play, combined with novel methods of making this truth felt by the audience.

What is the essential truth of a play? If it were possible to define it in precise terms, which everyone could understand and apply equally well, first-rate directors and first-rate critics would be commoner than

5

they are. The essential truth of any great work of art is elusive and may present itself partially, and in disguised forms, to many gifted seekers. The libraries of comment which have been written about one play alone, the tragedy of *Hamlet*, show us how hard it is for any single man to encompass the truth about it. Nor is it on the *Hamlet* level only that this problem presents itself. A theatrical director may make a botch of *Charley's Aunt* if he becomes convinced, let us say, that the important part of the play is the erotic frustration of old Mr. Spettigue. But if the director is an expert at his job, he will bring unusual qualities of insight and sympathy to his study of the play which he is to put on the stage; he will seize upon what is important in it, and he will find a way of imparting his conception of the play's real meaning to his audience.

But first he must impart it to his actors. How does he go to work?

There are directors who appear at the first rehearsal accompanied by an assistant who carries a very large book. In that book is the text of the play, and an elaborate mass of directions. Unless some crisis occurs, the rehearsals will be spent in teaching the actors to carry out those directions in the most minute detail, and no deviation from them will be tolerated. Some admirable work has been done by this method, but it is not the only method, and it is certainly not the most interesting method for the actors. It has advantages, from the director's point of view. Much of his work can be done by a trusted assistant. If his health is poor he can allow the assistant to give the orders, intervening himself only when he thinks it necessary. He may be absent from many rehearsals, especially during the early stages of work. With such directors,

6

the chief work of creation is done, not on the stage, but in the study. This method, the method of the *Regiebuch*, was brought to great perfection by the late Max Reinhardt.

At the other extreme is the director who appears at rehearsal with a thorough understanding of his play, and an idea for a production, but with no rigid notions as to how he is going to impart his understanding to the audience. He sets the actors to work, and as they work he improvises ceaselessly; he urges the players on to show him what they can do, and he makes use of whatever talents they bring with them, or uncover as they work. He builds up his production on the stage. His own concentration is complete and at rehearsal he is working at the very top of his form. Tyrone Guthrie belongs to this latter school of direction, and is perhaps the most interesting and exciting exponent of it today.

What happens at rehearsal? Let us see what we can do to call up the scene.

Rehearsal has been called for two o'clock. Half an hour beforehand the Stage Management has been at work, and the furniture and properties for the scenes which will be rehearsed are in place, or substitutes for them have been provided. The Stage Manager and one or two assistants are at a desk in the front row of the theatre, and one of them is, in the theatrical phrase 'sitting on the book'. Of course he is not really sitting on it; he is ready to prompt the actors. But the expression is a good one, for while he is engaged in that most ungrateful form of work, prompting, the man and the book are one. Actors who are not yet sure of their lines are often of explosive disposition, and it is the prompter's job to supply the missing word almost before the actor realizes that he has forgotten it. This is not so miraculous as it may appear. When an

7

actor's memory is failing him, his voice takes on a peculiar tone, not unlike that of a gramophone when somebody in another part of the house turns on the electric furnace. It is then that the prompter must speak out loud and bold. There must be no faltering, and certainly no scrambling to find his place in the text.

Being a good prompter is a gift, and a thing of temperament. Like good proofreaders, good prompters are men of a very special stamp, dedicated men, who know that they will never win any glory for themselves, and that they must get their satisfaction from saving the skins of others.

If the director is Guthrie, he is ready before the rehearsal hour, and most of the actors will be on hand, too. Some of them may have to be called from other parts of the building, but it is a rare thing for anyone to be late. These people are working, and they take their work seriously. An actor cannot do good work if he arrives just in time to begin, panting and flustered; calm concentration is the state of mind he seeks. The ones who arrive late are usually the younger members of the company, who have not quite grasped what a difficult job acting is, and how precious is every minute of rehearsal time.

The play itself dictates the tone of the rehearsals. If it is *The Shrew* the atmosphere is bound to be livelier, though not necessarily more interesting, than if it is *Oedipus*. But the rehearsal of a comedy is not a romp, during which the actors split their sides laughing at their own antics. Nor should anyone go to a rehearsal expecting to see something resembling a performance. With theatrical companies, as with orchestras, there is a technique of rehearsal which is quite unlike the technique of public performance. The rehearsal demands an incalculable amount of trial and error, of repetition, of minute alteration; the players must be ready to stop anywhere, and to repeat what they have done without loss of concentration, but with slightly altered effect. Lassitude, exasperation or displays of temperament even at one's own shortcomings, can have little part in this work, and are usually regarded as professional discourtesy. The concentration of rehearsal is different from that of performance, and may often be more intense.

Some directors work very well from an armchair, but Tyrone Guthrie is not one of them. He roams the theatre as he works, sometimes shouting his suggestions to the actors from the very back of the theatre, in an immense but carefully modulated roar; at other times he is right on the stage with them, demonstrating what he wants with broad gestures and occasional pushes and shoves, not unlike the presiding adult at a children's party. His descents upon the stage are sudden and often terrifying, though they are not meant to cause alarm. During rehearsals at the Old Vic before the War, when it still had an orchestra pit, it was not uncommon for him to put a foot on its brass rail, and reach the stage by a startling leap over that abyss. Dr. Guthrie is a very tall man, and a very strong man, and his physical feats have a strong smack of the prodigious about them which never ceases to alarm some timid souls.

It is this prodigious quality which stuns the observer when, on very rare occasions, he actually demonstrates to an actor what he wants him to do. There is a magnification about his gestures which I have never seen any actor successfully reproduce; nor is he meant to do so; he is expected to cut down whatever Guthrie has done to his own size.

9

Is Dr. Guthrie himself a good actor? The answer, disappointingly, must be both yes and no. He is a brilliant impressionist; he can convey the essence of what he wants in unmistakable terms, and he is a mimic of deadly skill; he reminds one of that actor described by Stephen Leacock, who could, in the absence of a table or a loaf of bread, give a striking impromptu performance as either. One of my cherished memories is of an occasion at the Old Vic, when *A Midsummer Night's Dream* was in rehearsal and the little ballet girl who was to play Mustardseed was absent; Guthrie solemnly played it, for that one rehearsal only, and very good he was. But it was what he himself would call 'untowardly casting'. And for a man of his stature most roles, except such occasional outsize parts as that of the Angel in *Tobias and the Angel*, are unsuitable. Sir Henry Irving turned his great height to good account, but Dr. Guthrie cannot be said to have done so.

He can act, and act very well, but he does not act very often at rehearsals. He prefers to get the actors to do his will by encouragement and exhortation. A director who cannot control his own passion to act is likely to be a time-waster. And if he is a good actor, he is likely to make all his company act like himself. Guthrie's desire is to find out what all the actors can do, and then persuade them to do it in the best possible way.

The rehearsal probably begins with a run-through of a scene which was worked on yesterday. This is not merely to warm the actors up; it is to see what they have added to it since last they worked on it before the director. They have not been working together, of course; they have probably not even been working, in the sense of moving, or repeating lines aloud, by them-

10

selves; but good actors are always working in that layer of the mind which lies just below consciousness, and when they have had a night's sleep between one rehearsal of a scene, and another, it is surprising how the scene will have 'jelled', and what qualities of depth will have been added to it.

Perhaps the director will let them play the scene to the end. Perhaps he will interrupt, and begin to rearrange it. This may take a great deal of time, and it is nothing to spend an hour working over a scene which may play for seven minutes in performance. But this is not wasted time, and no efficiency expert could speed it up. Such rehearsal as this is a search for the best, and that always takes time.

The rehearsal has not gone on for long before the interruptions of the director become frequent, the sound of the voice being preceded by a characteristic sharp clap of the hands. And we quickly realize that this handclap is not really to compel attention, for he has everybody's attention the instant he speaks. Nor is it simply a mannerism. It is a sound which in itself expresses the quality of these rehearsals, their intense concentration and alertness, their incisiveness and their high nervous pitch. These handclaps seem to mark the rhythm of the work.

Rhythm is a word which we hear again and again from the director. 'It's rhythm that does it, not energy', he cries at some young man who is trying to make his muscles carry him through a manoeuvre which is really a matter of relaxation and timing. 'The rhythm is *wrong*', he shouts at an actress who has not yet combined speech and movement in precisely the right way to illuminate a line of the text. Everything must be done and said at exactly the right moment, and a finished scene is an elaborate exercise in rhythm and cross-rhythm. It is this quality, perhaps more than any other, which makes Guthrie's productions so hard to reproduce. His famous Old Vic production of *The Country Wife* was taken to New York with its star, its magnificent designs, and a prompt-book with all the notes of Guthrie's production, complete. But Guthrie was not there, and the play did not last long when another director attempted to recapture what he had created. To reveal several thousand rhythms in a classical play is no small feat.

As well as rhythm, we also hear the word choreography, over and over again. This means something a little more complex than the successful moving of the actors around the stage. Choreography is particularly complex at Stratford, where the stage is observed by 1900 spectators, sitting in a semicircle. There are eight entrances from which actors can come, counting the trapdoor in the floor; there are a variety of levels upon which they can stand. They must present a good appearance from every part of the theatre at all times, and yet it is out of the question to pose them in pleasing tableaux. They must be almost constantly in movement. His skill in marshalling large numbers of people in fluid groups which are at all times related to the needs of the play is one of the things which marks Tyrone Guthrie as a master of his art. His choreography is not movement for its own sake, but a subtle physical expression of the mood of each scene—indeed, a dance.

There are countless stories about Guthrie's rehearsals, and people who have heard a good many of these sometimes get the impression that he works in an atmosphere of St. Patrick's day hilarity. Nothing could be further from the truth. It is true that if actors

12

named Hutt and House happen to be on the stage at the same time he is likely to refer to them as 'those two eminently desirable residences'. It is true that he may tell a stage full of actors who have worked themselves into an unfortunate grouping that they look like a bus accident. But he does not speak in this way with any particular desire to amuse, but because it reflects the colour and working of his mind, which is idiosyncratic, and marked by extraordinary flights from the apparently ridiculous to the sublime.

During rehearsals of *Oedipus* it was necessary for Donald Davis, who played the part of the prophet Tiresias, to fall upon the ground in a cataleptic stupor. This is not easily managed, the first time of trying. 'Ever seen a parrot faint?' asked Tyrone Guthrie, and when the actor said that he had not, he was given a short talk about the foolish temerity of parrots, and their habit of fainting when glared at by a cat. Thus instructed the actor found a way of falling to the ground which was deeply impressive. Of course this manoeuvre became known to the company as The Parrot Faint, but the important point is that Guthrie found a striking and evocative way of helping an actor to do the right thing, and what began as a parrot faint ended as something very different. It is not an ordinary mind which sees the connection between a fit of the vapours in a bird and the descent of divine truth upon a prophet. Yet it is this ability to see similarities between wildly dissimilar things which contributes to the imaginative insight of Guthrie's work.

It would be an error to labour this point with Germanic seriousness. But I must make it clear that what often passes for Guthrie's humour is not intended, primarily, as humour, but as an approach to truth.

13

And when truth is found in a grain of mustardseed we must either laugh or marvel—and it is embarrassing to everybody if we marvel too frequently.

It is also somewhat dangerous to marvel at Dr. Guthrie's brilliant strokes at his rehearsals, for actors who are admiring are not working, and he likes to see actors work. If they will not be coaxed, he is quite ready to drive them. When he is driving, stunning abuse and bad language ring from all parts of the theatre, as though an infuriated ventriloquist were at work; but it is all one man. Merciless, razor-like criticism cuts into the tumours which have developed on the scene under consideration; metaphorically, blood flows in buckets. One of these storms may impend, break and resolve itself into a dew as rapidly as the storm in the Overture to *William Tell*, but while it rages, everyone quivers. This is no mere stage thunder, worked up to impress; it is genuine wrath.

At the best of times Guthrie may criticize actors in terms which carry a certain sting, but they are not meant to hurt, nor do actors take them amiss. The skilful rider uses whip and spur without injuring the horse. Nor does any of this rebuke carry a personal edge; it is clear to the whole company that though he may, at times, loathe, execrate and despise them as actors, he is genuinely cordial toward them as human beings. Like those saints who, we are told, hated the sin while loving the sinner, Guthrie may easily hate what an actor is doing while keeping his respect and friendship for the man. Actors know this, and are often proud of drawing his fire. 'I was only called "stupid goat" three times this afternoon; I must be getting the hang of what he wants,' said one proud player after a long session of *The Shrew*.

14

Because I have dwelt at some length on the mercurial nature of Dr. Guthrie's directorial method, and the sharpness of his tongue, it must not be supposed that his rehearsals are exhibitions of slave-whipping and lion-taming. He is anxious to find out the utmost that every actor or extra in the crowd can contribute to the play, and then to see that it is all used in the best possible way. But his strongest interest is in the ensemble, and even when he is dealing with acknowledged stars of the stage he does not encourage star performances—in the sense of performances to which the legitimate importance of other roles is sacrificed. In this connection, by the way, it must be stressed that stars of the first magnitude are rarely as selfish as gossip and tradition has painted them. There are selfish stars, but it would probably be untrue to say that they are a majority among theatre artists of the first rank. Most of them are certain that they can hold their own, without selfish or unprincipled conduct, and it may be said here that the star players at Stratford have all been of this group.

The ensemble, then, is the important thing in a Guthrie production, and the ensemble is built up on intricate rhythm and choreography. It is a matter, also, of squeezing from the text every drop of meaning that it can be made to yield. It is for this reason that a very minor role, such as that of the Scrivener in the 1953 production of *Richard III*, may be thrust for a few minutes into prominence. The Scrivener's speech is easy to overlook, and easy to cut, for the sake of hurrying up the action. But the Scrivener has, in the light of the play as a whole, something important to say, and Guthrie sees that he has a chance to say it.

He is an expert, also, in establishing those relation-

15

ships which are implicit in the text, but which are
not noticed by every director. An instance of this
was the by-play which appeared in certain scenes of
The Shrew between Katharina and Hortensio; more
than once Hortensio showed himself an advisor to
Katharina by a nod or a gesture, or a glance, which
brought him fully into scenes in which he had few lines
to speak. These are things which it is very difficult to
arrange if the director is preparing the whole of his
production in his study, before he meets the actors.
But Guthrie's method is to work directly with the
actors, to try every possible scheme that will illuminate
the play, and to preserve what seems best from it all.
It is a method which gives each actor his due and
which has, over the years, given many a good actor his
first chance to show what he could do.

It is not a method which can be used by a director
who has not an intimate knowledge of the play, a
quick intelligence, and a fine classical sense of form.
Though the finished result, as with *The Shrew*, may
have the air of a happy improvisation, it is in reality
rooted at all times in the text, and the shape which
Shakespeare has given to the play is sternly insisted
upon. Indeed, in such a production this must be so, for
otherwise the play would vanish in a welter of tricks
and effects. And again I must return to the comparison
with music, for Guthrie frequently reveals that he is
thinking in musical terms.

He may tell his cast that the scene on which they
are working is a Coda—a summing up of what has
gone before, and in which therefore it is desirable to
give a display of technical brilliance, rather than a
sober statement of what is in the lines. Or he may tell
them that what they are doing is to be played at 'finale
pace', which is clear to anyone who has become

acquainted with classical opera. It is not by chance that Guthrie is a first-rate opera producer. He is sometimes astonished that actors do not fully understand him, for like many strongly musical people he finds it hard to remember that there are others who have little musical sense, and that a surprising number of actors are in this group. He also expects all actors to be able to sing—not, that is, to sing with professional excellence, but to be able to sing pleasantly and in a musician-like fashion. In this he is entirely justified, and there can be no doubt that acting on the whole would be greatly improved if all actors took the trouble to learn something about singing and about music generally. As Bernard Shaw never tired of pointing out, there is a musical counterpart for much of what happens in all plays of classical stature, and the actor who can sense this, and govern himself accordingly, may reach the truth by a valuable shortcut.

Guthrie's rehearsals appear to the casual observer to be endless exercises in detail. But the frame upon which all this detail will be hung is always clear in his mind, and it is clear to the actors, as well. The appearance of the horses in *The Shrew* is rehearsed again and again, so that their seeming wild scamper across the stage may be exactly right. The arrival of Old Vincentio's red limousine is worked over until it stops at just the right point, and so that the eventual piling-in of five actors (one of them Katharina in an elaborate gown) may be managed with the most apparent confusion, and the greatest actual dispatch. Embroidery hung upon a framework of steel—that is the lesson of every rehearsal.

If I have so far given the impression that Dr. Guthrie's rehearsals are a hubbub of excitement and handclaps, of wit, blarney and abuse, I must hasten to say at once that there comes a time, toward the end of the rehearsals, when he falls silent, and says very little. He gives notes at the end of each rehearsal, and the notes are principally about small things. But he watches all that goes on with deep concentration, and the actors are strongly conscious of him. Now, more than at any previous time, they are acting *for* him, and they know that if they win his approval they have succeeded, and no audience will have equal terrors for them.

In 1952 Dr. Guthrie gave a lecture before the Royal Society of Arts on play production, which has been printed, and in which he has some very interesting things to say about the director's function as 'an audience of one'. The director, who knows the play intimately, and who is deeply sensitive to the actor's part, is the man eminently worth acting for, and it is his commendation which, in the heart of the actor, must outweigh that of a whole theatre of others. And it is perhaps in these final rehearsals, by his expectant quietness and what he himself calls 'psychic evocation' in the address already referred to, that he does most. He demands every actor's best, and certainly in Canada it may be said that he gets it.

THE TAMING OF THE SHREW

By ROBERTSON DAVIES

THE TAMING OF THE SHREW

by WILLIAM SHAKESPEARE

(Characters in order of speaking)

CHRISTOPHER SLY	Robert Goodier
HOSTESS	Marionne Johnston
A LORD	Edward Holmes
1ST SERVANT	Roland Bull
2ND SERVANT	Neil Vipond
PAGE, as a Lady	Brian Gill
LUCENTIO, Suitor to Bianca	William Shatner
TRANIO, Servant to Lucentio	Donald Harron
BAPTISTA	Douglas Campbell
GREMIO, Suitor to Bianca	Eric House
KATHARINA, Daughter to Baptista	Barbara Chilcott
HORTENSIO, Suitor to Bianca	William Hutt
BIANCA, Daughter to Baptista	Frances Hyland
BIONDELLO, Servant to Lucentio	Douglas Rain
PETRUCHIO	William Needles
GRUMIO } Servants to Petruchio	Bruno Gerussi
CURTIS	Bruce Swerdfager
A PEDANT	Robert Christie
HABERDASHER	Peter Mews
TAILOR	Eric House
VINCENTIO	Lloyd Bochner
A WIDOW	Peter Mews
HORSES:	Warwick Butt, John Northmore
	Roland Hewgill, Orest Ulan

HUNTSMEN, SERVANTS, and CROWD: Charles Allen, Aimé Aunapuu, Valentina de Bruin, Neil Carson, Vincent Edward, June Faibish, Pauline Galbraith, Don Gollan, Jon Granik, Dawn Greenhalgh, Jack Hutt, Jim Jorgensen, James Manser, Walter Mills, Kenneth Pauli, Grant Reddick, Lois Shaw, Rose Mary Sowby, Mary Warren, Joan Watts, Jonathan White, Beverly Wilson, Clarence Wilson, Helene Winston.

DIRECTED BY TYRONE GUTHRIE
DESIGNED BY TANYA MOISEIWITSCH
MUSIC BY LOUIS APPLEBAUM
DANCES ARRANGED BY TOM BROWN

IF THIS PLAY is as bad as the critics say it is, why has it been so popular for 360 years? Why is it produced again and again today? A particular phase of public taste will keep a popular bad play alive for fifty years or so before the appetite for it wanes even among the most unsophisticated playgoers. But *The Taming of the Shrew* is one of the comparatively small number of Shakespeare's plays which has held the stage in one form or another since it was written. Let us look briefly at its stage history.

VERSIONS AND PERVERSIONS

THE USUAL date given for the original Shakespearean play (which he may have altered from another called *The Taming of a Shrew*) is 1594. Presumably it was popular and well-known, because in 1605 John Fletcher wrote a sequel to it called *The Woman's Prize, or the Tamer Tam'd*, which is about Petruchio's second marriage to a lady called Maria, who tames *him*. It contains references to the late, and apparently unlamented Katharina, and some descriptions of Petruchio's life with her. Tranio declares that—

> For yet the bare remembrance of his first Wife
> (I tell ye on my Knowledge, and a Truth too)
> Will make him start in's sleep, and very often
> Cry out for Cudgels, Colestaves, any thing;
> Hiding his Breeches, out of fear her Ghost
> Should walk, and wear 'em yet.

Unsuccessful plays never beget sequels in the minds of popular playwrights, and we may guess that Shakespeare's play pleased the crowd.

After the Restoration it appears again. That inveterate playgoer Samuel Pepys saw it, and thought it 'hath some very good pieces in it, but generally is but a mean play'. (He also saw *The Tamer Tam'd* and thought it 'a very fine play', a judgment which, like much of Pepys' drama criticism, suggests that his taste was not for all time, but of an age.) But what Pepys saw was in strict fact an altered version of Shakespeare, called *Sauny the Scot*, arranged by John Lacy. In 1715 two adaptations of the play appeared in London, both called *Cobler of Preston*, making much of the Christopher Sly elements in the original. In 1735 a musical version of *Sauny the Scot* called *A Cure for a Scold* was played at Drury Lane. It was a failure, but in our own time the musical comedy *Kiss Me, Kate* (first produced on December 30, 1948) has been a remarkable success, and it is probably no farther from Shakespeare than James Worsdale's eighteenth century flop.

GARRICK'S ABRIDGEMENT

IT WAS in 1754 that David Garrick, that shameless raider of Shakespeare's plays, produced a three-act version called *Catharine and Petruchio*. What he did, in effect, was to hack a 'starring vehicle' out of the original by removing all the sub-plot and the Induction. Christopher Sly vanishes, and with him go Vincentio, Lucentio, Gremio, Hortensio, Tranio and the Widow. It is interesting to notice that Garrick turned Curtis into a woman, and so persistent was this tradition that when the New York Theatre Guild produced Shakespeare's play in 1935, with Lynn Fontanne and Alfred Lunt in the leading roles, Curtis still was a woman. In the Garrick play Bianca's part is cut to a handful of speeches, and she is married off

ROBERT GOODIER
as CHRISTOPHER SLY
in *The Taming of the Shrew*
and as BARNARDINE
in *Measure for Measure*

to Hortensio. Nobody, in fact, has much to do except the leading actor and actress.

As Garrick did the adaptation, it is not surprising that Petruchio gets some of Katharina's best lines. By quoting the last few speeches from his version we may form an opinion of his method.

Baptista: Now fair befal thee, son *Petruchio*
The battle's won, and thou cans't keep the field.
Petruchio: Oh! fear me not—
Baptista: Then, my new gentle *Catharine*,
Go home with me along, and I will add
Another dowry to another daughter,
For thou are changed as thou hadst never been.
Petruchio: My fortune is sufficient. Here's my wealth.
Kiss me, my *Kate;* and since thou art become
So prudent, kind and dutiful a wife,
Petruchio here shall doff the lordly husband;
An honest mask, which I throw off with pleasure.
Far hence all rudeness, wilfulness and noise,
And be our future lives one gentle stream
Of mutual love, compliance and regard.
Catharine: Nay, then I'm all unworthy of thy love,
And look with blushes on my former self.
Petruchio: Good *Kate*, no more, this is beyond my hopes—
                 (*Goes forward with* Catharine *in his hand*)

Such duty as the subject owes the prince,
Even such a woman oweth to her husband:
And when she's froward, peevish, sullen, sower,
And not obedient to his honest will;
What is she but a foul contending rebel,
And graceless traitor to her loving lord?
How shameful 'tis when women are so simple
To offer war where they should kneel for peace;
Or seek for rule, supremacy, and sway,
Where bound to love, to honour and obey.

ADA REHAN AND JOHN DREW

THE GARRICK version is a shocking butchery of Shakespeare's play, designed to give all the 'fat' to Petruchio.

FRANCES HYLAND as BIANCA

Yet it held the stage for many decades, and there are many elderly playgoers still living who have seen it. Sir Herbert Tree used this text for his production in 1897. The first time that Henry Irving and Ellen Terry played together (at the Queen's Theatre, London, on December 26, 1867) it was Catharine and Petruchio in this abridged form. Shakespeare's play did not oust this intruder completely until well into the present century. The first production of the Shakespearean text that I can trace on the North American stage was Augustin Daly's in which Ada Rehan and John Drew were the stars; it was not what we should today call a full version, and Katharina's entrance in Act I, Scene 1, was cut in order that she might appear to greater advantage, tormenting her sister, in Act II, Scene 1; but the Induction was restored and Ada Rehan and John Drew were seemingly very fine. She played Katharina as a woman of great spirit, but of high breeding; at the end of her famous speech on the duty of women in Act V Scene 2, she used to give an almost imperceptible wink to her sister and the Widow, to suggest that her submission was not so complete as it might appear. Drew brought all his great store of grace and romance to the part of Petruchio, and though he carried the whip which the Garrick version had made obligatory, he is reported to have cracked it 'orchestrally'—which presumably means for emphasis, rather than as a threat. Drew and Ada Rehan appear to have been the first players to present Katharina and Petruchio as high-bred folk who took their strenuous courtship as a romp; this is the line which most modern productions follow.

WHAT THE CRITICS SAY

THE CLASSICAL Shakespearean critics have little to say about *The Taming of the Shrew*, and most of that little is derogatory or apologetic. The theatre critics of our day, writing of contemporary products, have little patience with it. 'Personally, I can't pretend to care much what anyone does with *The Taming of the Shrew*,' says Mr. T. C. Worsley, writing of the 1947 season at Stratford-on-Avon. Mr. Alan Dent dismisses it as 'this boisterous and dull farce'. Mr. Harold Hobson, writing of a production at Stratford-on-Avon in 1954 praises the performance, and continues: 'What more could one desire? Only, I suppose, a better play; or one less ignoble. I am amazed that those gentlemen who are so distressed at *A Streetcar Named Desire* or *A Day by the Sea*, or *Going To Town* being presented by a non-profit-distributing company should overlook such a piece of botched and revolting work as *The Taming of the Shrew* simply because it has a great name attached to it. There are four superb lines in the *Shrew*—something about a "waning age", something else about ne'er growing younger, something else still about peace and a quiet house, and a remark on rotten apples. For the rest it marks the absolute lowest ebb of Shakespeare's genius. Those four lines apart, there is more education, or semi-education, or whatever it is our watchful M.P.s want, in the final lyric Mr. Paul Dehn has written for the revue at the St. Martin's, than in all this dull, brutal, ill-written and indecent play.' This is con-demnation indeed, and the critic in the London Sunday *Observer*, writing of the same production, is almost kind to Shakespeare in comparison, when he writes of 'the crudity of the comedy, which is now as little liked as any in the canon'.

Before such literary fastidiousness and moral gran-deur as this we can but bow our heads in awe, recalling Sir Max Beerbohm's comment that the London critics, like the London Metropolitan Police, are a fine body of

ERIC HOUSE
as
GREMIO

Grant Macdonald '54

ERIC HOUSE
as the **COOK** and the **TAILOR**
in *The Taming of the Shrew*
and as the **JUSTICE**
in *Measure for Measure*

men. But we must still wonder why, if the play is so
bad, it has been so popular, in so many forms, for so
long?

WHAT THE PLAYGOER SAYS

THE ORDINARY playgoer, who has not the critic's professional interest in exhibiting himself publicly as a
Prodigy of Taste, can give the answer. The rowdy old
farce makes him laugh, and it satisfies something deep
in his nature. Petruchio exhibits a part of every man's
dream of himself—the triumphant woman-tamer. A
man may be on excellent terms with his wife, and with
all the women in his life, but he knows that he has—
however willingly—paid a price for that condition.
There have been times when he has reasoned, has
temporized, has held his peace. Doubtless he would
not have it otherwise. But it touches a thrilling chord
in his breast when he sees Petruchio showing one high-
spirited woman that another way—an ancient and
primal way—to domestic agreement is possible. Nor
does he miss the point that at the end of the play the
truest love is that between Petruchio and Katharina.

And what of this playgoer's wife? Does she resent
the play? Does she follow it with a burning eye and a
reddening cheek? No; on the contrary she enjoys the
spectacle of a man dominating a woman. She would
probably deny, if she were questioned, that she seeks
such a condition herself, but—she enjoys watching it
on the stage. And when, at the end of the play,
Katharina delivers her eloquent and beautifully
phrased harangue on the Duty of Wives, both the
playgoer and his wife seem perfectly happy. I have
seen *The Shrew* many times, and I have watched to
see if any couple left the theatre quarrelling. I have yet
to see this happen.

The most important part of Shakespeare's genius lay in his gift for piercing through the superficialities of our intellect to things which lie deep and secure in the human heart. I think that he has done this in *The Shrew*, and that its success and popularity are owing to the simple fact that it is a great play.

A GREAT FARCE

YES, A GREAT play, and one of the best farces in our language or any language. It is rough and bawdy, but where is it brutal? There is much in it that is condemned as buffoonery, by those who do not know how hard it is to write buffoonery on this level. Does anyone who has given five minutes of serious thought to the matter really suppose that it is easy to write a sure-fire farce? Does anyone really think that *The Shrew* is played again and again merely because Shakespeare's name is attached to it? If that qualification sufficed, why do we not see more of *Pericles, Titus Andronicus,* or *The Comedy of Errors?* No, *The Shrew* is buffoonery and farce touched by genius, and that is why it has held the stage.

It is the sex-war turned into drama. And if we watch the progress of the play, we cannot believe that Katharina is bullied into submission; her last speech, with its wonderful mixture of truth, and irony and blarney, is not the utterance of a woman who has been cowed, or who is hankering for revenge. The sex-war ends, as it always must if it is fairly fought, in a draw.

Is not this the inner truth of the play, which must strike home to the audience?

THE STRATFORD PRODUCTION

WHAT LINE WAS TAKEN with *The Shrew* in the Stratford Festival production of 1954? What was done to bring forward the old truth, and the old jokes, in a new guise?

Because the play was to be done in Canada Dr. Guthrie decided to give it what may be called, using the term very loosely, a North American setting. And thus we met the Lord, in the Induction to the play, with what might have been an autumn shooting party, for he and his friends carried rifles, wore mackinaw coats and field-boots, and had the air of men returning from our own northern woods. Christopher Sly, thrown out of the ale-house, looked like one of the late Walter Trier's wonderful tramps—most of all like Snuff, in *Dandy the Donkey*—and the ale-wife might have belonged to any time. But when the strolling players arrived, we were able to pin the time down rather more exactly; there were elements about them which suggested the beginning of the present century. When we moved into the Lord's house we found that his servants wore white coats and trousers—garments which suggested San Francisco, as much as they suggested anything. And when at last the play began, and Lucentio appeared in the white trousers, the blue jacket and the hard straw hat which suggested the great days of vaudeville, we felt that the brilliant sun of our West Coast was shining indeed.

THE ADVANTAGE OF MODERN DRESS

BUT IT is fruitless to try to assign a 'period' to this production. It had no period; it had only an atmosphere, and there is much to be said for producing a Shakespearean farce in this way. The clothing which we saw helped us to place the characters in the social scale. There was no danger of confusing Biondello, who was dressed as some mentally unstable sailor might, at some time before the First Great War, have

WILLIAM NEEDLES as PETRUCHIO

dressed, with Old Vincentio, who was clearly a pluto-crat. One of the troubles with Shakespearean produc-tions in seventeenth century costume is that we cannot always tell the gentlefolk from the servants, the old from the young, the fops from the austere; unless the designer is very careful they all present an appearance of fancy dress which muddles our understanding of the play.

The presentation of Shakespeare in modern, or fairly modern, dress presents some difficulties, of course. The fun with Bartholomew, the Page, did not come off too well in this production, though the part was well acted. But the atmosphere which worked so well most of the time failed in a few instances, and this was one of them.

The Shrew is a play within a play—a farce which the Lord hires the players to perform to amuse Christopher Sly. A neat illumination of the text was achieved in this production, through the use of a type of dress which the audience fully understood, which I have never seen brought off before. Speaking to the players, the Lord says:

> This fellow I remember,
> Since once he play'd a farmer's eldest son:
> 'Twas where you woo'd the gentlewoman so well.

He addresses this remark to the actor who later ap-pears as Petruchio, and sure enough, when Petruchio came on the stage at Stratford, he was 'a farmer's eldest son' to perfection, with his trousers tucked inside his boots, his collar visibly chafing him, a cow's-breakfast hat on his head and, above all, that air of being in town for the fair which suited the character that the director and the actor had contrived between them.

This may seem a trifling matter, but it is evidence

34

of the care which goes into a first-rate production of a Shakespearean play in what may be called 'modern dress'; the clothes in *The Shrew* were all very carefully considered and chosen for the illumination of character which they could give. The dandified Hortensio, with his pink shirt with white collar and cuffs; Bianca, in the garments of an Edwardian flapper; the maid-servants in the wedding scene (is there anything naughtier than four inches of white thigh above long black stockings?); the elegant motoring coat and grey bowler of Old Vincentio; the travel-stained 'duster' of the Pedant; Petruchio's Spanish hat and cloak at the end of the play, which turned him into an advertisement for a famous brand of port: these clothes were not *precisely* like anything in the heavens above, or in the earth beneath, or in the waters under the earth, but they made up a coherent whole, none the less, and they all bore directly upon Dr. Guthrie's basic concept of the production.

IMPROVISATION DEMANDS REHEARSAL

His IDEA was, apparently, to present the play as a wild improvisation—an extravaganza—to charm and delight the audience without consideration for time or place. And, like all improvisations which must be repeated over and over again, it was attached to an iron frame of discipline, and every seemingly fugitive effect was most carefully planned and rehearsed.

Because it achieved the effect of an impromptu, there were some spectators who thought that Shakespeare's text had been elaborately altered. But in truth nothing had been changed at all. Perhaps half-a-dozen unimportant lines were cut; another half-dozen at the very end of the play were slightly re-arranged, so that Petruchio's words—

35

DOUGLAS CAMPBELL
as BAPTIST
BARBARA CHILCOTT
as KATHARIN
PETER MEWS
as the HABERDASHE

DOUGLAS RAIN as BIONDELLO
BRUCE SWERDFAGER as CURTIS
DONALD HARRON as TRANIO
HELENE WINSTON as the COOK

'Twas I won the wager, though you hit the white;
And, being a winner, God give you good night!

should close the text was as we have received it from
the First Folio. The contemporaneous quality of the
play was overwhelmingly the work of that enduringly
contemporaneous writer, William Shakespeare.

WAS IT TRUE TO SHAKESPEARE?

WE MAY question, however, if Shakespeare's meaning
was followed as dutifully as his text. *The Shrew* is not
so brutal a play as the critics already quoted appear
to think. But it is not, on the other hand, a psychological study of shyness. As directed by Dr. Guthrie
this is very nearly what it became. We were shown a
Petruchio who was by no means sure of his power to
tame a shrew, and time and again in the production
we saw his valour oozing out at the palms of his hands.
He visibly summoned up his courage before every
determined action. He wore spectacles, and while
spectacles in real life are not specifically a sign of a
wavering spirit they are associated on the stage with
characters who are not especially courageous. There
was a hint of Harold Lloyd about this Petruchio which
was extremely amusing, but we were not so sure that
it was Shakespeare.

Katharina was conceived along similar lines. We
were given to understand that she was a frustrated,
nervous girl, whose dithering father and scheming
sister drove her to extremes of petulance. She never
faced Petruchio boldly; she, too, could be seen considering carefully before she made any move to cross
his will. Katharina and Petruchio were afraid of each
other.

This is ingenious and amusing, but it robs the farce
of some stature. When Ada Rehan and John Drew

38

played it, we are told that two raging fires met together—that the irresistible force and the immovable object were in head-on collision until the final scene. And, if a production so long in the past may not be adduced in evidence, let us consider the production in which Alfred Lunt and Lynn Fontanne made one of the great successes of their joint career. The present writer recalls it in detail. Who could forget the silky tones of that Petruchio when he assured Baptista that—

> I am rough, and woo not like a babe.

There was a wealth of promise—a whole soldier's biography in this line and the soft laugh which accompanied it. But neither the Stratford Petruchio, nor his Katharina, were permitted to appear as people of remarkable stature, and this is one of the faults of productions which insist at all times on ensemble effects. The bravura, the personal amplitude of Shakespearean leading characters may be diminished, and when this happens we cannot help but feel that the inner truth of the play has also suffered.

HOW WAS IT DONE?

BUT, SOMEONE may ask who did not see the production under question, how could this effect be achieved in the face of the repeated evidence in the text that Petruchio is a self-assured conqueror, and Katharina a 'hilding of a devilish spirit'? By a technical trick called 'playing against the lines'. The actor utters the boasts that Shakespeare has set down for him, but in such a voice, and with such hesitations and gestures as indicate that he does not fully believe what he is saying. This device is wonderfully effective when it is carefully used. But it can be used to excess, and it may be said that Dr. Guthrie is extremely fond of it. His

39

LLOYD BOCHNER as VINCENTIO
CHARLES ALLEN as his chauffeur

famous modern-dress *Hamlet*, in which Alec Guinness appeared in 1938, used this device so repeatedly in the leading character that we were very nearly given *Hamlet* without the Prince of Denmark. The effect was astonishing, and in some places it showed the text in an interesting new light; but the fact is that today it is the production which is remembered rather than the performance of the title role. That may be a very good thing, if ensemble effects are what please you most in the theatre. But we may question whether Shakespeare wrote with quite so much sacrifice to ensemble in his mind. He was, after all, an actor himself.

SUFFERINGS OF KATHARINA

IT COULD certainly be argued that Katharina and Petruchio were robbed of some of their splendours in this production, in order that an ingenious conception of their characters might be given a try. Of the two, Katharina suffered by far the most. It is extremely unlikely that the Petruchio Shakespeare has drawn would allow anyone to put insults upon his wife except himself. Yet this Katharina was pulled by the leg, slapped on the seat, trodden on, and spilled on, by her husband's servants until the effect was one of cruelty and dangerously close to degradation. And in the final scene of the play, when Katharina has her great speech on the Duty of Wives, this speech was interrupted and clouded by all kinds of directorial distractions, until the effect of it was almost ruined. It is questionable whether any good is done to a play by making the characters less than the author plainly intended, or by distracting attention from its proper focus at an important moment. It is sufficient that Katharina should be tamed; it is not necessary that she should be broken in spirit.

41

WILLIAM HUTT
as HORTENSIO
in *The Taming of the Shrew*
and as FROTH
in *Measure for Measure*

PERHAPS THE notion became prevalent that the text had been heavily adapted because the lines were spoken in a variety of contemporary accents, though not completely so. Once again, as with the costumes, this helped us to place the characters; Petruchio, the farmer's eldest son, spoke quite differently from the towny Hortensio, whose wonderful refinement in the line 'There's small choice in rotten apples', was one of the minor delights of the production. But there were difficulties. Baptista, played by an English actor, made no attempt to accommodate his speech to that of the others, and his daughters Katharina and Bianca spoke with accents which suggested that they had been brought up in quite different parts of Canada, and with only occasional visits to their father. Nor was it an entirely justified or happy inspiration to have Biondello follow his scrap of Latin—'cum privilegio ad imprimendum solum'—with the doubting interjection 'or sump'n'; it was funny, but a great part of the technique of the comedian is to know when he has been funny enough; Stephen Leacock has warned us against the temptation to be as funny as we can. There is much to be said for Dr. Guthrie's desire to present a farce in contemporary speech, but there is not absolutely everything to be said for it.

One point in particular needs to be stressed. The types of Canadian speech employed by many of the actors were thin and pinched in their vowel sounds, and careless of their consonants. Result: they were often hard to hear even when one sat close to the stage. Nobody wants to hear *The Shrew* spoken in the fruity tones of the nineteenth century elocutionist, but there is much to be said for a good, clear, speech untinged by any special regional accent. It is easy to hear, and

43

BARBARA CHILCOTT as KATHARINA

The Shrew is a play which seems to invite musical experiment, and the notion of getting the actors to provide the necessary accompaniment was a happy one and added greatly to the production's air of impromptu. Those who are interested in following up the matter of *Shrew* music (the whole subject of the music used, at various periods of taste, to accompany the plays of Shakespeare calls for an essay to itself) can still find old collections of songs in which passages of the text have been set by Sir Henry Rowley Bishop, to be performed by Katharina. One of these, called 'Should He Upbraid', was often sung by her as an introduction to the Wedding Banquet scene in the last act. And if it astonishes us that the taste of the mid-nineteenth century called for a musical Katharina, we may sober ourselves by wondering what will be thought, a century from now, of our demand at Stratford for a Katharina who performed a somersault that would have won the applause of a professional tumbler.

In the section of this book which deals with Rehearsal, mention has been made of Dr. Guthrie's fondness for musical terminology, and for dramatic effects which are akin to music. *The Shrew* provided one splendid example of what musicians call a disappointed climax. At the end of the Wedding Scene, Katharina and Petruchio have gone their stormy way, but the wedding guests remain, and the wedding feast is prepared. Baptista makes a weak attempt to create an atmosphere of gaiety, but his heart is not in the work. The party is flat, and even Lucentio and Bianca are subdued. They leave the stage with lagging feet and in disorder. It is clear that the wedding breakfast is going to be a miserable failure. So quietly does the scene end that the audience do not realize for a minute or so that an interval has arrived. We are used to some

46

EDWARD HOLMES as the LORD

flourish on the stage before we are dismissed.

The effect of the disappointed climax is to surprise, and if possible to shock. What we saw at this point in *The Shrew* was a Mozartian or Rossinian musical joke, transferred to the stage.

THE ACTORS

LET US turn our attention now to at least some of the characterizations which gave spice to this remarkable production. Some remarks have already been made about Petruchio and Katharina as they were conceived by the director; it was clear that the players had brought their skill obediently to the service of his conceptions, and had not attempted to enlarge or alter them in any serious respect. As I have tried to make clear earlier in this essay, both the virtue and the vice of the ensemble production lie in the necessity which is imposed upon everyone to work inside a frame which the director has made. But this is not to imply that such ensemble direction is a form of puppetry; if the director's conception is a large one, actors of large capabilities can work inside it very comfortably, and adapt themselves to it without doing any violence to their own artistic feelings. This is so in Canada to what may be an unusual extent, for though our Canadian players do not lack for ability, they are modest in their self-esteem, and follow direction very peaceably.

William Needles brought to the part of Petruchio a fine voice and a great deal of charm; he was entirely credible as the suitor who feels that he must overcome his natural diffidence, and dominate his bride. His moments of weakness were skilfully understated; he resisted the temptation to squeeze them for laughs, with the same artistic restraint which prevented him

48

from exploiting his charm of manner. His performance of Petruchio, within the bounds which Dr. Guthrie made obligatory, was full, eloquent, humorous, consistent, picturesque and continuously entertaining. This was a man, one felt, to whom Katharina would be obliged to forgive everything.

As the Shrew herself, Miss Barbara Chilcott was perhaps a little too sensitive—a little lacking in brass. This actress has the ability to convey fine shades of meaning very accurately, and she has a great deal of force when she needs it, but we missed the whirlwind quality which is necessary for Katharina. It is difficult to separate the director's concept from what the actress has done, and it may be that it was Dr. Guthrie's idea that this Shrew should be a girl of sudden but indecisive moods. Miss Chilcott gave us temper and at least one moment of high determination, when she shouted, 'I will be free!' in a voice which made the tent-poles shiver, but she never frightened us, and Katharina ought to have a dash of terror about her. But the director wanted a Shrew whose shrewishness was the outcome of nervous exacerbation, and that is what Miss Chilcott gave us. If it was not fully the Katharina of the text, neither was she playing with a Petruchio who was completely true to the text. But both these leading players fitted exactly into their places in the ensemble, and did what was required of them with abilities which went far beyond mere competence.

CANADIAN COMEDIANS

A REMARKABLE group of comedians showed us their paces in some of the secondary roles—comedians whose work should silence forever the suggestion that Canadians are without individuality in their humour.

49

Lucentio, the suitor of Bianca, is not ordinarily considered a comic role, except in the classic sense that all lovers who do not die are figures of High Comedy. But William Shatner brought some of the gifts of the vaudeville comedian to the part; his self-assured and somewhat brassy delivery of his first speech was in itself a pleasant bit of comedy, and all through the play he gave a dimension of comedy to a character which can very easily be a romantic bore. In the company of players who performed *The Shrew* at the Lord's bidding, his rank was obviously that of First Light Comedian, rather than First Walking Gentleman.

Indeed, all of the players in this production suggested very cleverly their status in the stock company, as well as the character which they played in the play itself. Douglas Campbell's brief vignette of an aging Tragedian and Heavy Father, and manager of the company, was charmingly observed, as were also the allurements which Miss Barbara Chilcott gave to the Leading Lady. Canadians who recall the many tours of one of our enduring Canadian travelling stock companies, that of the Marks Family, were pleasantly warmed when the Players made their first disordered but grandiose appearance.

As Tranio, the scheming servant, Donald Harron brought an unmistakable North American type to the stage; we doubt if Europe ever produced anything like this shrewd, impudent, yet craven and tremulous hobbledehoy, with a laugh like a whooping crane and a mouthful of buck teeth. Tranio is the Clever Valet of the old Italian Comedy; all of the characters in *The Shrew* are derived from that source. But this clever valet was no darting, lithe, backstairs Figaro, but a creature much nearer to our own time and our own

WILLIAM SHATNER as LUCENTIO

land—a clever man wrestling with a disabling gau-
cherie. It was a performance conceived and carried
out with unusual brilliance and sureness.

The resources of a small stock company do not
allow one actor for every part in a large cast, and we
have all seen such companies in which the doubling and
trebling of parts was common. Eric House, obviously
the Utility Man of this group of players, appeared
as the ancient Gremio in an outfit which suggested
Pantaloon; he gave the role a dignity which was not
unpleasing, and resisted the temptation to play for
pathos, though Gremio might legitimately do so. His
lines—

> My cake is dough: but I'll in among the rest,
> Out of hope of all, but my share of the feast—

are surely quite as good as those which appealed to
Mr. Harold Hobson, and there is a dash of elderly
philosophy in them which is very appealing. But as an
effeminate Tailor, Mr. House achieved a fine mingling
of comedy and pathos. The Tailor has been played in
all sorts of ways, and it is not uncommon to play him
with a stutter, or with very bad eyesight, or some comparable affliction. But as Mr. House played him he
was a creature denied full manhood, but not without
dignity and integrity. It was very funny, but it was not
cruel.

Nor was there any cruelty in William Hutt's portrait
of Hortensio, though this part of the rejected suitor
can be made ridiculous. Hortensio, as we saw him, was
a monster of refinement—a smartly dressed, affected,
but very likeable fellow. His disguise as Licio the
Musician turned him into a back-street Paganini, a
shaggy virtuoso in a seedy woollen jumper; he even
attempted to capture some of the famous *terribilita* of

Paganini, but his own foolish good-nature kept peeping through the disguise, with rich comic effect.

A LINK WITH COMMEDIA DELL' ARTE

A FINE CONTRAST to this fine-feathered Hortensio was Douglas Rain's creation of a Biondello who seemed always to be grappling with the mere power of speech. As Biondello is a very eloquent servant, this was an amusing and novel effect; talk bubbled out of him like soda-water from a bottle, yet he was never in full command of it; he wore the worried look of a man who is perpetually groping for the next twenty words. A link between *The Shrew* and the Commedia dell' Arte is the long set speech, the burst of descriptive eloquence with which Biondello describes the approach of Petruchio to his wedding. As played at Stratford, this was a notable ensemble effect, in which the whole stageful of people staggered under the scatter-shot of Biondello's verbal assault, sinking at last into exhaustion. This display of fireworks was in excellent contrast to Biondello's other famous speech —the one about the wench who went to the garden for parsley to stuff a rabbit—which was given in short spurts, as he toiled up the steps toward the most remote of the Stratford stage exits.

Another characterization which was very much of our time and country was Bruno Gerussi's creation of a tough, back-alley Grumio, tireless in self-excuse, ingenious in gesture and mischief. He wore a look of cynical resignation, and he moved as if the atmospheric pressure upon him were at least double that experienced by an ordinary human being. He was a rascal, this Grumio, and not an entirely pleasant rascal. It is not uncommon to see these Shakespearean rascals played as though, in spite of their behaviour,

53

butter would not melt in their mouths; it is as if the
actor were determined to show that he is really a very
decent chap, and is only pretending to be a rascal for
fun. But Bruno Gerussi gave us a Grumio whose
rascality was in the grain; it would endure wind and
weather.

A CUP-SPRUNG PEDANT

THE PEDANT of Robert Christie was one of the
delights of the production, for it seemed to create a
small island of serene happiness in a world that was
full of feverish hubbub. The Pedant was drunk. Of
course the Pedant is always drunk in productions of
The Shrew. But this Pedant was gloriously, enchanted-
ly drunk; in him drunkenness had produced a kind of
seedy sainthood, an all-embracing generosity, a slop-
ping over of the milk of human kindness. Why is the
Pedant a pedant? Presumably this is another echo of
the play's derivation from the old Italian Comedy, in
which learning was thought to be hugely comic. We
rarely see anything in a production of the play which
suggests that the Pedant knows more than how many
beans make five. But Robert Christie's Pedant was
fully credible as a man of learning; his exuberant
urbanity suggested that rare type, the man in whom
learning has produced honey without a trace of gall.
When, as the False Vincentio, he teetered perilously
on the parapet of the Stratford balcony; when, in the
confusion of a street-fight, he was almost carried aloft
by his own umbrella; when, his deception being dis-
covered, he left the stage like a benevolent worm,
virtually on his belly—all these manifestations told us
of a man who used his learning to bring sunshine into
the lives of the unlearned, and who asked nothing in
return save a constant supply of something—anything
—potable. This was comic acting on a very high level.

BRUNO GERUSSI
as
GRUMIO

A PLEASANT BIT of doubling was done by Peter Mews, as the Haberdasher and as the Widow. The Haberdasher is a one-line part. But when this Haberdasher appeared in a messenger-boy's suit with rose-pink facings, and a pill-box hat he fully achieved his purpose, which is to draw from Petruchio a storm of abuse. As the Widow the actor had a better chance. Dr. Guthrie has a fondness for casting men in this part; indeed, the present writer may claim to have been Dr. Guthrie's first male Widow, at the Old Vic in 1939. It may be that men understand the psychology of this role better than women; this is not the place to argue the matter. But Peter Mews made a Widow of admirable delicacy of manner, and with just the faintest hint of a whisky voice. His appearance was a pleasant surprise near the end of a play which was a procession of surprises. After all, Shakespeare wrote his women's part for men and boys, and in 1922 Dame Ellen Terry declared that a boy whom she saw play Katharina in a school production of *The Shrew* was better than any woman she had ever seen, barring only Ada Rehan. The boy was the 15-years-old Laurence Olivier.

A FRENCH BAPTISTA

IT REMAINS only to say that Douglas Campbell brought his rich comic skill to the part of Baptista, who appeared at times to be drawn from the theatre of Labiche, rather than that of Shakespeare; smoking his hooked pipe, dressed in a blue smock and sheltered from the sun by an ancient panama, this was the perfect figure of a French bourgeois papa. As his younger daughter Bianca, Miss Frances Hyland played with a delightful mingling of sweetness and calculating mischief; it was part of the director's conception that Bianca should be more of a shrew, but cleverer at concealing it, than her sister. Miss Hyland gave us a charming picture of an Edwardian flapper, and her indelicacies at the wedding banquet were both satirical of the new-found liberty of the recently married, and indicative of an impending problem for young Lucentio.

VINCENTIO THE PLUTOCRAT

AN ADMIRABLE comic performance, all the more interesting because it came from an actor whom we do not normally think of as a comedian, was that of Lloyd Bochner as the plutocratic Old Vincentio of Pisa. His arrival in a red limousine (preluded by cries from under the stage of 'Ahoo-gah! Hoo-gah!' which we were presumably to accept as the noise of a klaxon) was a fine surprise. But tricks do not make a play. It was Old Vincentio's dismay at being greeted as a 'Young, budding virgin, fresh, and fair, and sweet', and his deflation when this was corrected to—

This is a man, old, wrinkled, faded, withered—

which delighted us, and his acceptance of the subsequent explanations was a wonderful study of a rich man taking a joke. That this part, with its few lines, stands out in the memory, is a tribute to the truth and imagination brought to it by this admirable actor. And, we may ask, in how many theatres in the world are so many excellent actors ready to give excellent performances in secondary roles as at Stratford?

THE CROWD

IT WOULD be ungrateful indeed to mention the actors in this production without saying a special word about the admirable contribution of the crowd—those hunts-

57

men, servants, policemen, wedding guests, photographers, and others who did so much to give life and richness to the play. One of the virtues of a first-rate ensemble production is that it permits fine crowd effects, and Dr. Guthrie is a master in creating and incorporating such effects into his work. Who that has seen it can forget that wonderful scene of expectant wedding guests, thrown alternately into ecstasies of anticipation, and abysses of despondency? Who can forget the wonderfully doleful cook, who sought to extinguish a loaded pistol by stamping on it? Or the optimistic girl who, after the painful anticlimax of the wedding whirled her rattle hopefully, just to see if something of nuptial gaiety might not be recaptured? These fugitive delights, though in no sense a part of Shakespeare's play, were very much a part of this concept of it, and we were grateful for them.

SLY AND HIS HOST

Nor may we forget the figures of the Induction, the Lord and Christopher Sly. The Lord is an ungrateful role, but Edward Holmes lent it a fine presence and an air of detached attentiveness which were very valuable. And as the beguiled tinker, Robert Goodier contrived to be lovable without ever sinking to mere sweetness; his astonishment, his concern, his desire to interfere in what he saw, were wonderfully valuable to a play which, without this framework, loses its best reason for being. It was a fine moment when, at the end of the play, the Lord covered his strange guest and, after paying off the players, bade him a silent goodnight. In *The Taming of a Shrew*, from which Shakespeare drew some of his material for his own play, Sly is thrown back on the heath, where he wakes, and determines to hurry home to do a bit of shrew-taming

ROBERT CHRISTIE as the PEDANT

himself. It is a good ending, though a little too prolonged for modern taste. The Stratford conclusion in
pantomine has a charm which is very welcome at the
end of a strenuous evening.

A COLLECTOR'S PIECE

WHAT ARE we to think of this performance? It was
immensely enjoyable and yet, in recollection, it seems
to have lacked certain elements which we may fairly
expect from so good a production of *The Shrew*.
Originality and wit in its conception, technical skill
and inventiveness in its execution, a classic beauty of
design underlying the elaborate ornamentation of its
rhythm and choreography—it had all of these splendid
qualities. It was successful in one of the most desirable
and most difficult feats of comedy production, in that
it swept the spectator into a world which was complete in itself, with its own laws and conventions, and
in which the commonplace considerations of every-day
probability had no part. Yet there was a driving
quality, a nervous and restless forcing of the pace all
through the play which left us as much exhausted as
delighted. We were conscious of yearning for a little
more charm, a little more—no, not sentimentality, but
sentiment. This world which had been so cleverly
created for us lacked a dimension of humanity; it
lacked a depth of humour. Argument on this point
could be greatly prolonged, and the critic can only put
forward his own feeling, hoping that some other playgoers will, if they do not agree with him, at least
understand the point that he is trying to make.

But no one who saw *The Shrew* at Stratford will be
sorry. It was, in its special way, a wonderful experiment, and for those who try to see as many Shakespearean productions as possible it was a collector's
piece of rare quality.

60

MEASURE FOR MEASURE

By ROBERTSON DAVIES

MEASURE FOR MEASURE

by WILLIAM SHAKESPEARE

(Characters in order of their appearance)

VINCENTIO, the Duke	Lloyd Bochner
ESCALUS, an Ancient Lord	Mavor Moore
ANGELO, the Deputy	James Mason
ATTENDANT	Jonathan White
LUCIO	Donald Harron
1ST GENTLEMAN	Neil Vipond
2ND GENTLEMAN	Roland Bull
A YOUNG LORD	William Shatner
COURT CHAMBERLAIN	Neil Carson
MISTRESS OVERDONE	Marionne Johnston
POMPEY, Servant to Mistress Overdone	Douglas Campbell
THE PROVOST	Robert Christie
CLAUDIO, a Young Gentleman	Douglas Rain
JULIET, Beloved of Claudio	Barbara Chilcott
FRIAR THOMAS	Edward Holmes
FRIAR PETER	James Manser
ISABELLA, Sister to Claudio	Frances Hyland
FRANCISCA, a Nun	Eleanor Stuart
JUSTICE	Eric House
ELBOW, a Simple Constable	Peter Mews
FROTH, a Foolish Gentleman	William Hutt
ABHORSON, an Executioner	William Needles
BARNARDINE, a Dissolute Prisoner	Robert Goodier
MARIANA, Betrothed to Angelo	Toby Robins

NUNS, CITIZENESSES, Etc.: Aimé Aunapuu, Elizabeth Barry, Valentina de Bruin, June Faibish, Pauline Galbraith, Dawn Greenhalgh, Jo Hutchings, Olga Landiak, Patricia Powers, Edna Pozer, Lois Shaw, Rose Mary Sowby, Lucille Walker, Mary Warren, Joan Watts, Lynn Wilson, Helene Winston.

GUARDS, JAILERS, PRISONERS, CITIZENS, Etc.: Charles Allen, Warwick Butt, Neil Carson, Vincent Edward, Bruno Gerussi, Don Gollan, Jon Granik, Roland Hewgill, Jack Hutt, Jim Jorgensen, Walter Mills, John Northmore, Kenneth Pauli, Grant Reddick, Bruce Swerdfager, Orest Ulan, Beverly Wilson, Clarence Wilson, Donal Wilson, William Lang.

DIRECTED BY CECIL CLARKE
DESIGNED BY TANYA MOISEIWITSCH
MUSIC BY LOUIS APPLEBAUM

The setting for the song 'Take, Oh Take Those Lips Away' is by Cedric Thorpe Davie.

THE SPECIAL TRIUMPH of the Stratford Festival of
1953 was a production of *All's Well That Ends Well,*
which did much to illuminate and reveal the beauty of
that somewhat neglected play. In the 1954 Festival
another of Shakespeare's 'difficult' plays, *Measure for
Measure,* was offered, and proved popular. It requires
courage to present these plays, because they are not
well known to playgoers, and people who pretend to
know what the public likes often say that the public
does not like them. But the public at Stratford has
liked both of these plays very much, which at least
suggests that both plays are strong stage pieces when
they are well cast and understandingly presented. Yet
a mystery hangs about them, and there is perhaps no
play which leaves the critics so much at a loss as
Measure for Measure.

A PUZZLE FOR THE CRITICS

INDEED, criticism of the play is scant, and throws
little light upon it. Shakespearean scholars are pretty
well agreed that the text of the play which we possess
is a severely cut and patched version of a longer and
presumably more coherent original. But this alone
does not explain the queerness of the play, and the
disagreeable impression it has made on many people
of fine taste; and we may not wave aside several
important critics just because we do not agree with
them. Dr. Johnson thought that it was 'darkened' by
what he called 'the peculiarities of its Authour'. Coleridge called it 'a hateful work, although Shakespearian
throughout'. Swinburne says that the audience is

'defrauded and derided and sent empty away'. Those of us who enjoyed the play at Stratford, and found it deeply satisfying, are neither obliged to contradict these great judges, nor need we feel that we are creatures of poor taste because we do not agree with them. We may say, however, that Johnson and Coleridge and Swinburne appear to have formed their opinions in the study, whereas we formed our own by watching an excellent stage performance—and after all, Shakespeare wrote the play to be seen, and not torn to pieces by critics. But I hope that readers may find it interesting if we take some time to look closely at the play, in an attempt to find out what it is about and why, though we enjoyed it, we found it something of a puzzle.

IS IT REALLY A BOTCH?

THE PLAY was written about 1603-4, and this means that it was a product of Shakespeare's greatest period. Look at the chronology of these seven years:

1601. *Julius Caesar*
      Hamlet
1602. *Troilus and Cressida*
1603. *All's Well That Ends Well*
      Measure for Measure
1604. *Othello*
1605. *Timon of Athens*
1606. *King Lear*
      Macbeth
1607. *Anthony and Cleopatra*
      Coriolanus

Here is much of Shakespeare's finest work, including the five great tragedies and four plays which have been called sour, embittered and disillusioned. Are these plays comparatively failures, produced by an extremely uneven workman? We can take the easy

64

JAMES MASON as ANGELO

way, and suppose that Shakespeare, exhausted after the supreme achievement of *Hamlet*, wrote muddled and indifferent plays until he hit his stride again in *Othello*. But we may also, and I think more wisely, assume that at least part of the failure may lie in our understanding of these difficult and seemingly repellent plays, and that they are not the fag-ends of the playwright's genius, but aspects of it which we must puzzle over until they yield up part of their secret.

Let no reader suppose that I hope to reveal everything that the greatest Shakespearean critics have failed to find. But there are ways of examining works of art, and particularly works of literature, which are available to our age which were not available to Dr. Johnson or even to Swinburne, and although we must not ride the hobbies of our time too violently, we would be foolish to neglect means of investigation which lie ready to hand.

A HELPFUL CRITICAL APPROACH

ONE OF the most interesting and revealing pieces of Shakespearean criticism to appear in our time is a series of essays on *Hamlet,* written by Dr. Ernest Jones, president of the International Psycho-Analytical Association, and a critic of great penetration and intuitive power. It would be far outside the purpose of this book to summarize Dr. Jones' theories here, but he lays great stress on the influence of the death of Shakespeare's father in 1601 upon the writings of the poet during the next few years—the years which produced the great tragedies and the bitter comedies. Discussing *Measure for Measure,* one of the great Shakespeare scholars of our time, and of all time, Sir Edmund Chambers, says, 'Upon the causes of this new perturbation in the soul of Shakespeare it is perhaps

66

idle to speculate.' Nevertheless, Dr. Jones speculates upon this theme at length, and to good purpose. He answers questions which have stumped other critics and throws light into many dark places.

Following in the footsteps of Dr. Jones, another psycho-analytical critic, Miss Ella Freeman Sharpe, has written a study of Shakespeare's later plays which, though far from carrying full conviction to the mind, contains much that is of interest and helpful in our consideration of *Measure for Measure*.

In reading what follows, I must ask you to bear in mind that I do not set up to be a psycho-analytical critic. I have not the training for that work, and any such pretension on my part would be inexcusable impudence. But I have attempted to read *Measure for Measure,* so to speak, by the light of Dr. Jones' torch; I make no claim to have read all that a critic deeply skilled in this type of criticism might read, but as no critic whose work I can find has tried this method, I shall do my best, hoping that I may cast some fitful gleam upon the perplexities of this strange play.

THE PLOT

BRIEFLY SUMMARIZED, *Measure for Measure* is about a Duke of Vienna who pretends to leave his city, having deputed his power to Escalus and particularly to Angelo, a man of admired virtue. But the Duke does not go away; he stays in Vienna, disguised as a friar, to spy on his subjects and his deputies. Angelo revives an edict against fornication, and the first offender, Claudio, is condemned to death because he has seduced Juliet. Claudio's sister, Isabella, is about to become a Sister of St. Clare; she goes to the deputy Angelo to plead for her brother's life and he, falling in love with her beauty and goodness, offers to release

67

Claudio if Isabella will be his mistress. Isabella plots with the Duke to trick Angelo and pretends to yield to him under circumstances which make it possible for a rejected betrothed of Angelo's, named Mariana, to take her place in Angelo's bed. The Duke then pretends to return to Vienna, deals out a stern measure of justice to all offenders, and announces his intention of marrying Isabella.

FACTUAL TRUTH OR POETIC TRUTH?

IT IS NOT ENOUGH to say that this is simply one of the involved Italian tales which Elizabethans enjoyed, and that its characters are pasteboard. Shakespeare dealt with several such stories, and when he had done with them the characters were never left as puppets. And the behaviour of several of the people in *Measure for Measure* is puzzling, though when we see the play acted we accept it and are caught up in their struggle. We are, indeed, persuaded to set aside our doubts and questions for the duration of the drama, and to believe in what we see, and think it important. Would we do this if the play were merely a dramatized Italian tale to which nothing had been added? It is not reasonable to suppose so. Is it not the case, rather, that this play has a poetic truth which is more important than mere superficial credibility—that it appeals to something in us which demands satisfaction, but does not necessarily also demand a story which would be believable as a newspaper report?

Scholars must endlessly *explain* Shakespeare; audiences find it enough to *feel* the impact of his plays. And the scholar must explain Shakespeare in terms of the scholarly mind, which is not by any means always the same thing as the poetic mind. The behaviour of the Duke in this play, and the behaviour of

68

FRANCES HYLAND as ISABELLA

Isabella, strain scholarly credulity, for they do not behave as scholars imagine that reasonable (that is to say, scholarly) people must behave. But if we simply accept the play, as an audience does, interesting and potentially helpful reflections begin to break in upon us.

WHO IS THE DUKE?

THIS DUKE, for instance—who and what is he? He is called Vincentio in the Cast of Characters, but this name is never used to address him or speak of him. He is invariably called The Duke, and he stands for absolute power in Vienna. He pretends to leave his city, but in reality he remains in it, disguised; he says that he has given power to Angelo, in order that Angelo may enforce strict laws that the Duke has allowed to lapse, but the reasons he gives in support of this are not completely convincing. We believe him more readily when he says that he wishes to see if power will corrupt Angelo.

Is the Duke simply a coward, who fears to do what he should do, and who sneaks in disguise to spy on a man he has loaded with honours and compliments? No, the character does not appear in this light. But we are given a hint that he is a man who likes disguise and mystification, for does not Lucio speak of him as 'the old fantastical duke of dark corners'?

What are we to think of a man as aloof, as withdrawn, as fond of mystery and what he calls 'the life removed', as this Duke? What do we make of the fact that he is plainly eager for social reform, but that he chooses to bring it about indirectly, and as a power behind the throne, rather than directly, and with full honour and blame upon himself? A psychiatrist, encountering such a man as this Duke, would lose no time in recognizing him as a man with a well-established God Complex, for he exhibits a large number of the classical symptoms of that cast of mind.

Whether the Duke is merely a man who identifies himself with God, or whether he stands as a symbol for God in the play, we cannot determine, but when, in the last act, he reappears in Vienna in his own guise and deals out justice to all comers, he bears a powerful resemblance to the character of Divine Correction in the medieval morality plays. And, if he is so nearly allied to God, we find it easier to understand Isabella's strong attraction toward him, and her willingness to do what he wishes, even when it is such an ambiguous trick as the substitution of another woman for herself in the bed of the seducer Angelo, in order to cheat Angelo of a promised favour. Isabella is on the point of taking her final vows in a religious sisterhood; she is, in fact, about to become a bride of the Church—a woman wholly obedient and devoted to God. How seriously she regards her pledge we may judge from her comment to the nun Francisca that she desires 'a more strict restraint upon the sisterhood'. No demands of God can be too strict for Isabella.

But is this not to be explained simply as religious fervour? Why should we assume that Isabella's obedience to the disguised Duke is anything more than a devout novice's obedience to a worthy friar?

THE BITTERNESS OF ISABELLA

WE MAY best attack that problem by considering one of the most interesting and theatrically effective scenes in the play—that in which Isabella explains to Claudio that Angelo will spare him if she yields her body to Angelo's desire. Claudio knows that death awaits him, and the Duke, in his friar's gown, has exhorted him most eloquently to accept death with resignation. When Isabella comes to him she urges him further to face death bravely, and when he boldly declares that he will do so she praises him in these significant words:

> There spake my brother: there my father's grave
> Did utter forth a voice.

There is no doubt that, in Isabella's mind, everything that is noble and honourable is associated with the memory of her dead father; nor need we look very far to see instances in which a living brother is invested in his sister's mind with the authority of a dead father. Thus it seems to be with Isabella.

But when Claudio learns that there is a way in which he can escape death, and that his life may be purchased by his sister's sacrifice of her virginity, he pleads very movingly with her to take that step. She then turns upon him:

> O, you beast,
> O, faithless coward, O, dishonest wretch,
> Wilt thou be made a man out of my vice?
> Is't not a kind of incest, to take life
> From thine own sister's shame? What should I think?
> Heaven shield my mother played my father fair . . .
> For such a warped slip of wilderness
> Ne'er issued from his blood . . . Take my defiance,
> Die, perish . . . Might but my bending down
> Reprieve thee from thy fate, it should proceed . . .
> I'll pray a thousand prayers for thy death,
> No word to save thee.

These are hard words indeed, and many critics have quoted them against Isabella. Why could she not, they ask, have made this sacrifice to save her brother? In Maeterlinck's play *Monna Vanna* the heroine makes the same sacrifice in order to save the people of Pisa,

72

LLOYD BOCHNER as the DUKE

and we love and honour her for it. This girl, who can
say:

> Then Isabel live chaste, and brother die;
> More than our brother is our chastity—

is, to put it mildly, not very likeable, and when she
seems perfectly ready to marry the Duke at the end of
the play, without any suggestion of courtship between
them, we are apt to wonder if she has not been saving
her virginity as her contribution to an advantageous
match.

But immediately this thought crosses our minds, we
recall that she has no thought of marriage, other than
her marriage to the Church. Isabella is affianced to
God, and she docilely accepts the Duke. Is the Duke
a surrogate for God, as Angelo is a surrogate for the
Duke?

ISABELLA AND HER FATHER

SOME LIGHT is shed on this question when we examine
Isabella's cruel speech to Claudio. She says, in effect:
'I hope that my mother did not betray my father when
she conceived you, but you do not behave yourself like
his son.' Her father bulks so powerfully in Isabella's
mind that she jealously disparages her mother's
honour, when Claudio fails to behave like this beloved
father; this father is so much her ideal of manhood
that, when Claudio fails to be like him, she accuses
him of being the son of someone else. And, in the line
which precedes this bitter outburst, she speaks of
incest. It does not take any very remarkable insight to
perceive that Isabella is in love with her father, and
loves Claudio only insofar as he serves as a substitute
for that father. She is affianced to God, it is true, but
the alliance between the father-figure and the concept
of God in the unconscious mind is widely recognized.

74

And thus her quick alliance with the Duke, who takes God-like attributes upon himself, and who appears to her in the guise of a friar—a 'father' in the sense that all priests are 'fathers'—seems less extraordinary than it did.

THE OMNISCIENT DUKE

IT CANNOT be said that the Duke fails to play the part of a father to Isabella. He makes plans for her, which she is ready to carry out without a moment's questioning, devious and unsavoury though they appear to us. The Duke's pretensions to omniscience would be shocking if he did not carry them off with so much self-assurance; he says, at the end of the play, that he has taken confession from Mariana, and knows her virtue; has he really assumed the prerogatives of priesthood, along with his friar's disguise? This is the act of a fantastical duke of dark corners indeed. But the Duke makes another reference to confession, earlier in the play, and opens up a curious avenue of speculation.

In the scene referred to above, in which Isabella rejects Claudio's pleadings and speaks so bitterly of her mother, the Duke intervenes between the two, and tells Claudio that Angelo never meant to harm his sister. 'She, having the truth of honour in her, hath made him that gracious denial which he is most glad to receive: I am confessor to Angelo, and I know this to be true.' Now, on the face of it, this is a flat lie; the Duke is *not* confessor to Angelo, and knows nothing of the kind. But who is Angelo? Is he not the Duke's surrogate? Does he not act upon the Duke's authority, and stand for him in Vienna? Has the Duke not said to him:

In our remove, be thou at full ourself.

Is not Angelo, perhaps, an extension of the Duke's own person—another aspect of the same man?

75

Certainly, if this were the case, the Duke might fittingly declare that he has knowledge of what is in Angelo's mind which would otherwise be available only to his confessor.

THE DUKE AND HIS SURROGATES

THE OBJECTION will be made at once that the Duke gave his power not into the hands of one surrogate, but of two. We must not forget old Escalus, that personification of charity and common sense. Angelo has been quick to condemn Claudio for fornication. But in that wonderful court scene where Angelo leaves Escalus to deal with the case of Master Froth and Pompey Bum, we find a curious parallel to the main action of the play, presented to us in a miniature of low life. The constable, Elbow, hales Pompey and Froth into court, complaining that when Madam Elbow, longing for stewed prunes, sought them in the Bunch of Grapes, Master Froth made some attempt upon her honour. Whether or not he was successful we shall never know, for the evidence presented is as confused as police court evidence can be, but we receive the impression that Madam Elbow did not escape with her honour unscathed. And Escalus, considering the nature of the persons involved, and the nature of the evidence, and the very harmless character of Master Froth's face, dismisses them all with a warning not to let it happen again, and gives Pompey some good advice, which that resolute bawd declines to take. What Shakespeare intends us to understand from this we cannot finally decide, but we have seen the only moderate and intelligent handling of justice that appears in this strange play, in which, Sir Edmund Chambers remarks, 'the searchlight of irony is thrown upon the paths of Providence itself'. We all hope that,

DOUGLAS CAMPBELL as POMPEY

if we must be judged, we shall be judged by an Escalus, and not by an Angelo or a Duke Vincentio. If the Duke is Providence, as well as Isabella's ideal of a father, and if Angelo and Escalus are other aspects of his nature, we may say that Escalus represents charity and simple human goodness.

ISABELLA AND PATIENT GRISELDA

WHAT, THEN, is Angelo? Leading actors often prefer this part to that of the Duke, because Angelo has at least two fine scenes in which he is allowed to show a soul at war with itself. But we must not be blinded to the fact that, at the end of the play when everybody is judged and punished by the Duke, Angelo is let off rather lightly; he suffers some humiliation, and he is married to Mariana—not a hard fate, considering that his sin was that for which he had condemned Claudio to death. Angelo's purpose in the play seems to be to test the chastity of Isabella, and we must see that the person to benefit chiefly from her survival of this test is the Duke, who makes her his own.

Nor is this the only test that is laid upon Isabella. We cannot forget that strange scene in which the Duke, knowing full well that Claudio is alive, tells Isabella that—

His head is off and sent to Angelo.

He does this, so far as we can judge, for no better reason than to see how she will take the news, and to prepare the way for his great effect when he produces Claudio alive.

In the relationship of the Duke to Isabella there is more than a trace of the story of Patient Griselda, in which a woman is humiliated and overborne, simply to see how she will take it, by a man who values utter

78

MAVOR MOORE as ESCALUS

subjection in a wife. We cannot escape the feeling that the Duke and Isabella, when once they are married, will set up one of the most richly neurotic households of all time.

THREE FATHERS

BUT LET US return to the puzzle of the Duke, and his two deputies, Angelo and Escalus. If *Measure for Measure* were a dream, instead of a play, a psycho-analyst would say that these three men are all aspects of a single man, and that single man is a father-figure, as a father appears in the mind of childhood; the supreme and arbitrary power of a father resides in the Duke, the wisdom and tenderness of a father are found in Escalus, and the rival in love is found in Angelo who attempts to come between Isabella and her affianced bridegroom. And, as dreams and works of art have much in common, such speculation is not unhelpful in prying into the conundrum which is *Measure for Measure*.

SHAKESPEARE AS SON AND FATHER

WE HAVE already taken note of the fact that this play was written directly after *All's Well That Ends Well* in which play the heroine, Helena, stands in an interesting relationship to another father-figure, the King of France, and wins her husband by a trick very much like Isabella's. The power of fathers appears to have been very much on Shakespeare's mind at this time, and *Hamlet* is not the only play in which it appears. It has been suggested by Sigmund Freud and Dr. Ernest Jones that the death of Shakespeare's father in 1601 had a profound effect upon the poet, and it is clear to any student of the plays that Shake-speare, from 1601 until at least 1608, was passing

80

through a period of deep disillusion and discourage-
ment which was at odds with his worldly success. Ella
Freeman Sharpe, in a group of essays which were
unfortunately not finished at the time of her death in
1947, has advanced a theory of cycles of depression
and elation in Shakespeare's work, and *Measure for
Measure* lies midway in one of the descents. But must
we assume that Shakespeare's own father is the sole
inspiration for these problems which attach to father-
figures? Was not the poet himself a father? In 1604,
when *Measure for Measure* was written, his elder
daughter Susanna was twenty-one; it is of interest that
she married a physician, John Hall, (who had settled
in Stratford in 1600, when Susanna was seventeen);
Helena, in *All's Well*, is a gifted physician; Hall was
a sufficiently distinguished physician to be summoned
forty miles from Stratford to Ludlow, to attend the
Earl and Countess of Northampton. Is it extreme to
suggest that the presence of Hall as a suitor (he
married Susanna in 1607) may have begotten in the
poet's mind something of this tangle of father-
daughter relationships which we find in these two
plays?

But this is for someone else to investigate; this book
has no space for such byways of speculation, however
tempting they may be. We must leave this subject with
the reflection that the last of Shakespeare's plays, *The
Tempest*, tells of a father and daughter, plainly revealed in their relationship, and in a thorough and
happy mastery of life.

A BAWDY PLAY

ONE ELEMENT in this play still calls for comment. It
is the bawdiness which, here, goes as far as in any play
in the canon. The plot and dialogue of *Measure for*

Measure are shot through and through with sexual references, implications, evocations and jokes on every level, and the fun ranges from the genuine wit of Lucio to the rich dirt of Pompey. It is not enough, as Eric Partridge has pointed out, to say that Shakespeare put such matters into his plays to amuse the groundlings; the bawdry in *Measure for Measure* is in the grain of the work, and to be honest we must assume that Shakespeare liked it, wanted it and needed it.

DAS EWIG-WEIBLICHE

NEVERTHELESS, the harping on sex and the sexual act in this play is by no means all funny. Isabella's attitude toward her chastity is in deadliest earnest, as Claudio had cause to know. But what is this chastity upon which she sets such store? Is it simply 'to have the body in the soul's keeping', in Blake's phrase? No; chastity which is valued above a brother's life is something more than that. Chastity which goes so far places an abnormal and suspect value upon the sexual act. And, in the light of what has been said about Isabella heretofore, the reader who agrees with my view of her will further agree that Isabella's fierce chastity is another aspect of her love for her father; there is no talk of chastity from her, or of her nun's vows, when she is claimed as his own by the father-Duke. And this brings us once again to the theme of incest, of which psycho-analytical critics have made much in their considerations of Shakespeare. Is the poet's unconscious incestuous wish directed toward his mother, as is suggested by *Hamlet*? Or toward his daughter, as is suggested by the foregoing examination of this play? In the psycho-analytical point of view mother and daughter figures in the unconscious mind

DONALD HARRON
as
LUCIO

often merge one into the other. 'Das Ewig-Weibliche zieht uns hinan' in Goethe's summing-up.

And there we must leave it. Readers who do not like it are free to discard it. But in defence of these random and imperfect reflections upon this strange and admittedly difficult play I may say that they provide a logic for the behaviour of some of the characters which is not easily found elsewhere; they throw some light on the curious conduct of the Duke, and the apparent ferocity and unsympathetic behaviour of Isabella toward her brother; they suggest why Angelo does not receive a heavier punishment for his attempt upon Isabella's virtue, which contrasts so strangely with the hard fate of Lucio. They explain, in my opinion, why we accept as poetic truth things in this play which are against all ordinary credulity, and excuse conduct which is in the ordinary way inexcusable. For poetic truth is a different thing from factual truth: the latter speaks to the surface of the mind, and the former to those deeps of the mind in which our emotions and our most cherished beliefs have their roots; poetic truth gains acceptance in those regions where itself came to birth, and Shakespeare speaks from the depths of his mind to echoing depths in his audiences.

THE PRODUCTION

THE STRATFORD production of *Measure for Measure* was mounted with dark splendour. The prevailing colours in the costumes were black, grey and silver, and in the large stage pictures lighter colours were sparingly used to provide relief and emphasis. The Duke was at all times a dominating figure, whether he wore the white robe of Friar Lodowick or his splendid robe of state and justice. But what is conceived as a picture is not always kind to individual characters. Escalus, for instance, wore colours which were in excellent contrast to the heavy black of his fellow-deputy Angelo, but which gave a factitious air of elderly vanity to the character. Isabella's dress, though suitable to a novice in a nunnery, was not helpful to the actress at moments when it was necessary for her to dominate the stage. When the stage was filled with people, these costumes took their places beautifully as parts of the visual effect, but as aids in the creation of character they were less successful.

The pageantry and choreography of the production was striking and appropriate; the atmosphere of court, of street, of prison, was created at once, without needless elaboration and yet without scamping. The severity of the Duke's regime was suggested by soldiers in black and silver armour, carrying huge halberds; the majesty of that regime was expressed in a great double-headed eagle, borne on a pole, which was the first and the last thing to be seen in the performance. The rough-and-tumble of the street scenes was suffi-cient to suggest the pulsing, close-packed life of a great city, and Mistress Overdone's coop of ruffled night-birds, and the young gallants who resorted to them, were in evidence without being intrusive. And again, in the prison, we saw enough of the foul and ailing jailbirds to rouse sympathy and curiosity, but never so much that we could be sure of what we had seen. This capacity for allusion and suggestion marked the production at every turn, and it formed an interesting contrast to the explicit statement and elaboration of the other two plays in the festival. In *Measure for Measure* it was splendidly effective to deal thus in hints and half-revelations, for that is the character of the play.

THE PLAY demands three actors of star rank in the roles of Angelo, Isabella and the Duke, but these performances must rest upon a good ensemble, and the festival company was well able to provide it. Modern audiences are far more critical of the ensemble of a production than they were, for instance, when the late Robert B. Mantell used to visit Canada, and astonish us with performances of his own which had flashes of excellence, and even of greatness, but which were given against a background of actors who ranged from mediocrity to ineptitude. This company could provide Mavor Moore to give weight and consequence to the role of Escalus; this wise old councillor must be credible as a trusted deputy of the Duke, and a fitting colleague for Angelo; it is a part which, while not large in itself, can do much to give quality to the sum of the production. A similar addition to the whole was made by Robert Christie, as the Provost, that steeled gaoler who befriended his prisoners. William Needles, capable of giving us an excellent Petruchio in *The Shrew,* brought the same talents to the very small part of Abhorson. Shakespeare illuminates that part with only one considerable line, but it is a beauty: 'A bawd sir?' cries this hangman, when offered Pompey as a helper, 'fie upon him, he will discredit our mystery.' It was good to have that line delivered with the weight of a star behind it. And Barnardine, that strange prisoner, sodden with drink and overgrown with hair like the Count of Monte Cristo, was played by Robert Goodier with a fine dignity and, strangely enough, with a kind of romantic dash. It is one of the virtues of repertory that actors of this quality can be used in small parts, in which they add strength to a production in the place where, under ordinary circumstances, it is most likely to be weak.

86

TOBY ROBINS as MARIANA

THE PLAY was well served, also, in its scenes of low life, which are vital to it. It was one of the producer's many good strokes to let us see something of that Mistress Kate Keepdown, to whom Lucio is finally mated, and this silent role was sufficiently but not obtrusively sketched in by Jo Hutchings. Marionne Johnston gave us a Mistress Overdone who was not the bawdy-house keeper of tradition—fat, debauched and careless—but a woman with the cares of an endangered business on her mind, a woman custom-shrunk and in retreat before the powers of righteousness. The worried Elbow was played by Peter Mews, who has a special gift for depicting mental confusion. Shakespeare does not appear to have had a high opinion of policemen; he regarded them much as did Sherlock Holmes. As we saw Elbow, shambling and hangdog, carrying a spiky but futile club and with a face which seemed to have run entirely to nose, he was the perfect picture of the Scotland Yard bungler. Yet there was a charm about him, too, and his protests in behalf of his own good character, and that of the wronged Madam Elbow, were genuinely touching.

As the accused in this case, the taciturn and wayward Master Froth, William Hutt created from very little material a character which lingers in the mind and gives deep retrospective pleasure. This actor has an uncommonly expressive face. It is not that he makes faces, but rather that his face mirrors with considerable subtlety every thought which crosses his mind. As Froth he stood in one spot, leaning somewhat out of plumb, and gave us, through the medium of his face, an astonishing number of variations on the theme of self-satisfaction. He was pleased to be arraigned for having offered attentions to the constable's wife; he was pleased to stand revealed as a man with four-score

88

PETER MEWS
as
ELBOW

pounds a year; he was pleased to have the harmlessness of his expression adduced as evidence in his defence: he only ceased to be pleased once, and that was when the death of Froth the Elder was mentioned; at that moment a spasm of melancholy passed fleetingly across that mask of tipsy well-being, as a wisp of smoke may drift across the face of a lamp. This performance of Froth was a notable miniature.

But the comic scenes in this play rest chiefly upon Pompey, and while Douglas Campbell did not give us the whole of Pompey he gave us most of him. Pompey is an amusing villain, but he is a villain none the less. The actor gave us one flash of the complete Pompey at the end of the court scene, where he disappeared down one of the tunnels with the defiant words—

> Whip me? No, no; let carman whip his jade:
> The valiant heart's not whipt out of his trade—

and as he vanished from sight he gave a prodigious heave to his codpiece in which all of the cynical brutality of Pompey was displayed. This was a fine moment, and we felt the lack of others to match it. But the actor brought a fine unction to the role, and a wonderful power to depict dismay, as when he staggered back from the stench that arose from the dungeons.

Good as the individual performances were by the actors who played the low-life parts, there was a lack of power in the whole which weakened the production. In *Measure for Measure* we sense the corruption of a city; the Overdones and the Pompeys and the Keepdowns and the Froths are the lesser creatures who fatten upon the vices of such men as Lucio. If we are not given a strong sense of this vicious and festering life, the action of the Duke and the severity of Angelo are not sufficiently set off. One of the points in

90

DOUGLAS RAIN as CLAUDIO

which this production failed to satisfy us was in the suggestion of vice and corruption on a large scale. The low-lifers, excellent as individuals, had not been used in such a way as to suggest a dukedom with its foundations in a dungheap.

CHARACTERS OF HIGH LIFE

IT WAS from Lucio, played by Donald Harron, that we received the strongest suggestion of a corrupt state. Lucio is a dangerous man. He is witty, excellent company, and his malice is amusing; he is so attractive, indeed, that we very often forget that he is a lecher, a slanderer and a man capable of infinite mischief. In a curious passage of criticism Bernard Shaw speaks well of Lucio, because he has good manners, and speaks to Isabella and Mistress Overdone in different vocabularies; but Lucio's fatal vice is that he will say anything at all that will contribute to his momentary importance, and such people are more harmful than many thorough-paced villains. The festival production was fortunate in having for this part an actor who could bring to it not only physical grace and charm, but a thorough understanding of what makes Lucio loathsome. Mr. Harron very nearly succeeded in doing, single-handed, what the low-life characters had failed to do because they possessed too much charm and good nature. Professional voluptuaries, and those who minister to them, are not invariably people of golden heart and overflowing good nature, whatever sentimentalists may choose to think, and Shakespeare was no sentimentalist. This player showed us not only the attractive side of Lucio, but also the cynical disregard for truth, the hypocritical esteem for virtue (when it happened to reside in a young and beautiful virgin) and the uncurbed egotism of the man. This was a piece of acting which brought distinction to the whole play.

Lucio is attractive vice; Mariana is scorned virtue, and the actress who plays her has little to do except be beautiful and allow the audience to project its own favourite conceptions of virtue upon her. Miss Toby Robins is admirably suited to a role which demands beauty, but it must be complained that in this production she was not given the benefit of all the beauty that Shakespeare had contrived for her.

Shakespeare never used music loosely. It is always introduced into his plays with a purpose, and when first we see Mariana, one of his most beautiful lyrics is sung, certainly to enhance the romantic melancholy of her situation. For this production 'Take, Oh Take Those Lips Away' had been charmingly set to music by Cedric Thorpe Davie, but the song was so raggedly and quaveringly sung by a group of young women behind the scenes that it almost entirely failed of its effect. We could not hear the words, and what we did hear sounded like sight-reading by a girl's school mastering the tonic sol-fa. There is no reason why Stratford, thoroughly professional in everything else, cannot rise above a bad amateur level in the performance of its music. Actors who can sing, and even sing unaccompanied, are surely not impossible to find? The directors of the plays should rely more upon their musical advisor, for these descents into amateurism dispel atmosphere and—as in this case—spoil effects which Shakespeare has taken pains to provide. When Mariana was free of her household glee club she was well able to fill the place in the play which the author had given her.

With Juliet, as with Mariana, appearance is of first importance, and Miss Barbara Chilcott had no trouble

93

MARIONNE JOHNSTON as MISTRESS OVERDONE

in showing us the unfortunate lady, Claudio's companion in an indiscretion which circumstance turned into a crime. She was particularly effective in the prison scene in which she learns that her lover must die; here, once again, was justification of a system which makes actors fully capable of large parts occasionally available for small ones.

THE PROBLEM OF CLAUDIO

CLAUDIO, for reasons which have been touched upon in the consideration of the play at the beginning of this essay, is a difficult part, for he must fill at least part of the role of hero, without having anything heroic to do. He appears first as a convicted seducer, which is an undesirable, though perhaps not irreparable, handicap if he is to gain the full approval of the audience. We sympathize with him when he appeals to Isabella to take the course which will save his life, but when she gives him her famous tongue-lashing, he has no satisfactory reply. Even at the end of the play, when Claudio is released, his sister gives him no greeting, though it is usual for the director to manage an embrace between the two; it would be interesting to see a production in which Isabella does not greet Claudio, but nurses her bitter grudge to the end; it would be perfectly in character for her to do so. The plain fact is that we have a sense that Claudio is an important character, but he is not given much that is important to do. Therefore the actor must somehow manage to make bricks without straw, and to impress Claudio upon us by force of personality. This Douglas Rain was fortunately able to do. He gave Claudio a dignity in misfortune which commanded our pity, and he spoke his famous speech about the terrors of death with a degree of imaginative power which was one of

95

LLOYD BOCHNER as the **DUKE** disguised
ELEANOR STUART as **FRANCISCA**
ROBERT CHRISTIE as the **PROVOST**
JAMES MANSER as **FRIAR PETER**

JAMES MASON as ANGELO
OLGA LANDIAK as the MOTHER SUPERIOR
JONATHAN WHITE as an ATTENDANT

the high points of the production. Claudio is one of the ungrateful parts which Shakespeare—or whoever prepared the cut-down versions of some of his plays which are all that we now possess—gave to actors without much apparent thought as to what can be made of them in performance. In this instance the actor was able to make a fully rounded figure from the outline provided in the text.

THE FANTASTICAL DUKE

THE STAGE HISTORY of *Measure for Measure* shows us that leading actors have never fully made up their minds as to whether the principal male role is the Duke or Angelo. The Duke is showy; he is on stage a great deal of the time; he has several fine speeches; he is permitted to display a variety of moods. Yet, the Duke never completely commands our sympathy, and much of the drudgery of the play is allotted to him; he does a great deal of the laying-out of the plot, and there is something rather undignified about the way in which he scampers through the play, tampering here and interfering there until, when he tells Isabella that her brother is dead, merely to see how she will take it, we are out of patience with him. Shakespeare has given the Duke too much power, and too little humanity, for him to be wholly likeable. Thus we may say that the actor who gets this part gets a plum, and a great deal of hard work, and a problem, all in one.

The problem is to give the Duke humanity. There are opportunities for this, as when Lucio slanders the disguised Duke to his face; Lloyd Bochner, who played the Duke at Stratford, seized upon these opportunities, and did a great deal with them. He also made the Duke a rather better actor than noble amateurs

98

NEIL VIPOND as the FIRST GENTLEMAN

usually are; as Friar Lodowick his gait and countenance were surely like a father—as Shakespeare says in another place. We admired this meddling friar, whenever we could forget that he was the all-powerful Duke in disguise, and Mr. Bochner made it easy for us to forget. He brought great gifts to the role, for he has a fine voice and a superbly handsome presence, in addition to the intelligence which illuminates everything he does. The leap from Vincentio the Duke in this play to Vincentio the plutocrat in *The Shrew* is a great one, but this actor managed both with fine command and authority. His delivery of the Duke's great speech on Death was one of the high spots of the production, and he contrived the plot with Mariana in a way that gave no suggestion of a sanctified Pompey— a very considerable feat. If Shakespeare meant the Duke to represent Providence, he gave Providence some uncommonly shady work, and it is the actor's job to make us swallow it. For sheer acting virtuosity this performance exceeded anything else in the production.

ISABELLA

As the devout Isabella, Frances Hyland had to overcome physical difficulties which stood between her and that very difficult young woman. Miss Hyland is of small stature and her personal attraction is better described as charm than as allure; it is easier for an actress whose figure and voice contradict Isabella's religious aspirations to get away with some of Isabella's curious behaviour. We feel that Isabella is a woman of emotion, rather than intellect, and Miss Hyland suggests intellect and reason. To put it in operatic terms, Isabella is a contralto role, and Miss

Hyland is a soprano. Because of this lightness and vivacity of personality, Miss Hyland was sometimes sharper than Isabella should be, and at the first performance her celebrated outburst against Claudio came perilously close to scolding.

But it is not the purpose of this book, which has the advantage of considering these plays in retrospect, to judge upon first night performances, and the first night of *Measure for Measure,* which was also the first night of the festival, showed no one to greatest advantage. When the festival got into its stride, all the plays changed somewhat in character. *The Shrew* lost shrillness and gained charm; *Oedipus* lost something of its impressiveness and in some roles a painfully perfunctory quality asserted itself; but *Measure for Measure* gained in depth and strength until, by the end of the festival, it was better in every respect than it was at the beginning.

There was growth in Miss Hyland's performance. She became softer, yet stronger, as Isabella, and she found places where a relieving womanly tenderness could be given expression. She settled into the role, and broadened her emotional conception of it, until we felt that Isabella's actions were not the expression of a somewhat embittered mind, but rose from the depths of her being, and expressed uncontrollable emotional needs.

It is such growth as this that divides the artist from the lesser player. There are theatre-goers who assume that each succeeding performance is a decline from the standard achieved on the first night. Too often experience supports this point of view. But the artist-actor creates freshly at every performance, bringing new experience and new insight to it until it is ripened. That is what Miss Hyland did with Isabella.

ROLAND BULL as the **SECOND GENTLEMAN**

THAT IS what James Mason did, also, with the part of Angelo. His first night performance suffered from an inhibiting nervousness, which particularly affected his voice, robbing it of sonority. He was plagued by misfortunes which no one could control, including train whistles and the roar of aeroplanes, whose salute to the occasion unfortunately coincided with one of his first important speeches. Only those who have had some taste of public appearance know how disconcerting these things can be. But as the festival progressed his performance was revealed as a deeply-considered, subtly imagined study of a man at war with himself— a powerful and moving piece of acting.

Angelo has been played in many ways—as the man of ice who melts before Isabella's beauty, as the hypocrite who checks his lust in order to deceive the world, as the puritan whose creed is at odds with his desires —but Mr. Mason gave us an Angelo more subtle than any of these. Here was a man genuinely good, though not wholly good; here was a man deeply ambitious, yet with a fine integrity and sense of justice; here was a man against whom ordinary temptations would have been powerless. It seemed to me that the key to this characterization lay in the lines—

> O cunning enemy, that, to catch a saint,
> With saints dost bait thy hook!

This Angelo had much of the saint in him, and his struggle was not a war in which gratification of lust lay on one side and power and reputation on the other, but a conflict between frightening desire and genuine virtue.

Having taken this line, it was not altogether easy for us to swallow the story of the cast-off betrothed,

Mariana, into whose arms Angelo is betrayed. But Mr. Mason's conception is consistent with the text, and we were content to let the Mariana story pass by without too much examination, in order that we might enjoy this fine performance and believe in it. The actor brought great intensity, and great inner power, to his character, and when the anxieties of the first night were over he gave it a suitable and individual vocal performance.

A MOVING FAREWELL

ANECDOTES are easily overdone in any book about a theatrical venture, but sometimes they support a point not otherwise quickly made. Let it be recorded here, therefore, that Mr. Mason's final appearance as Angelo was the occasion of a powerful and heart-warming demonstration of respect and affection for him, on the part of the audience and his fellow-actors. Nor was it only for the spirit which he showed in joining the festival company; it was a tribute to an actor of fine abilities who had put those abilities at the service of two great plays. There could be no doubt about the sincerity of feeling which was shown during those few minutes in which the actor took his public leave of the festival.

THE PRODUCTION VINDICATED

SOME MURMURS were heard, during the 1954 festival, about the inclusion of *Measure for Measure*; this play, and *The Shrew*, it was hinted, were lightweight choices for a festival in which Shakespeare was to be the principal offering, and enquiries were made as to when one of the big tragedies would be attempted. Now it is true that Stratford will have to face the test of one of Shakespeare's great tragedies sooner or later,

but the people who brush *Measure for Measure* aside
as of slight account in the Shakespearean canon had
better think again. It is one of Shakespeare's 'difficult'
plays; it takes courage to produce it at all, and skill
to produce it as well as this. In its first two years Stratford has shown its quality by tackling, in this play and
All's Well That Ends Well, two plays which are not
among the sure box-office successes, and drawing full
and enthusiastic houses to see them. This is not evading the task of a Shakespearean festival, but meeting
it head-on. *Measure for Measure*, in the form in which
we have it, is a damaged masterwork, and if the Stratford venture is to make Shakespeare known to thousands of Canadians it must show us such plays as this,
as well as the popular comedies and the acknowledged
great tragedies. The courage of the festival in choosing
the play, and the artistry with which it was done were
matched by the receptiveness and appreciation of the
audience.

OEDIPUS REX

By ROBERTSON DAVIES

OEDIPUS REX

by SOPHOCLES

in a version by W. B. Yeats

(Characters in order of their appearance)

OEDIPUS	James Mason
PRIEST	Eric House
CREON	Robert Goodier
TIRESIAS	Donald Davis
JOCASTA	Eleanor Stuart
MAN FROM CORINTH	Douglas Campbell
OLD SHEPHERD	William Needles
MESSENGER	Douglas Rain
CHORUS LEADER	William Hutt

CHORUS: Robert Christie, Donald Harron, Peter Mews, Bruno Gerussi, Grant Reddick, Roland Bull, Neil Vipond, Neil Carson, Jonathan White, James Manser, Edward Holmes, Bruce Swerdfager, William Shatner, Roland Hewgill.

NURSE	Marionne Johnston
ISMENE AND ANTIGONE,	Lois Shaw and
daughters of Oedipus	Valentina de Bruin

ATTENDANTS ON CREON: Warwick Butt, Vincent Edward, Jon Granik, Jack Hutt, Jim Jorgensen, John Northmore, Orest Ulan, Beverly Wilson.

SUPPLIANTS: Aimé Aunapuu, Elizabeth Barry, Barbara Colley, Beatrice Dabbs, Isobel Dickson, Carole Ernest, Marilyn Ernest, June Faibish, Pauline Galbraith, Dawn Greenhalgh, Olga Landiak, Margaret Hall, Jo Hutchings, Doreen Jackson, Patricia Powers, Edna Pozer, Anne Pritchard, Marie Shackleton, Rose Mary Sowby, Lucille Walker, Mary Warren, Joan Watts, Lynn Wilson, Sandra Wilson, Helene Winston, Charles Allen, Bob Barr, Robin Freeman, Don Gollan, John Mair, Walter Mills, Newman O'Leary, La Verne Palmer, Kenneth Pauli, Clarence Wilson, Donal Wilson.

DIRECTED BY TYRONE GUTHRIE
DESIGNED BY TANYA MOISEIWITSCH
MUSIC BY CEDRIC THORPE DAVIE

Masks designed by Tanya Moiseiwitsch and Jacqueline Cundall

THE DECISION TO include Sophocles' *Oedipus Rex* in the 1954 festival at Stratford was fateful, for it dispelled one of the shadows which had been hanging over the venture—that shadow of second-rateness which dims the lustre of all imitations. True, no one pretended that the Canadian festival rose to the stature of an imitation of the festival at Stratford-on-Avon during its first year, but it would quickly have met with all the problems of an imitation if it had not asserted its individuality quickly. At a place named Stratford, what would it be but a Shakespearean festival? And, in a British Dominion, how could it escape the charge of imitating the greatest of all Stratfords? And, branded as an imitation, how could it ever hope to be judged fully on its merits? By making it clear that it was not exclusively Shakespearean, the festival took the most important step toward meeting all these difficulties, and it was a great piece of good fortune that, of the three plays seen in 1954, *Oedipus Rex* was the most completely successful. Stratford has claimed the freedom to move where it pleases in the realm of classic drama. No doubt there will be years in the future when it will choose to perform Shakespearean plays only, but it will be a choice, and not an obligation.

The performance of *Oedipus Rex* in 1954 was a triumph for all who were concerned with it. There is plenty of room for dispute about it, and those who did not like it were able to bring strong arguments to bear against it. But I doubt if anyone can maintain successfully that it was not a complete and magnificent creation within the limits which it established for itself, or that these limits—though we may not like them all—were not themselves nobly conceived.

PROBLEM OF GREEK DRAMA

It is often said that great difficulties lie in the way of those who would bring Greek drama to the modern stage, and this is true enough. But we may wonder whether these difficulties have not been exaggerated to a degree where they look deceptively like impossibilities. Within the memory of the present writer, two great productions of *Oedipus* have been seen by Canadian playgoers. The first was Reinhardt's production of the play in Gilbert Murray's translation, with Sir John Martin-Harvey in the principal part; the other was the Old Vic's production, under the direction of Michel Saint-Denis, which many Canadians travelled to New York to see during the summer of 1946; in it Sir Laurence Olivier played Oedipus. Both of these productions, performed in theatres of the conventional nineteenth century design, with a picture-stage, were dramatically powerful and deeply moving. They did not give us the play as the Greeks of the fifth century, B.C., knew it, but what of that? Neither has anyone within the past century given us *Hamlet* as it appeared to the London playgoers of the early seventeenth century. But can we truly say that the *Oedipus* or the *Hamlet* that we see is better or worse than the original performances? Can we honestly say that the version of *Oedipus* which Dryden wrote for his late seventeenth century audience, with its subplot and its—to our ears—stilted verse, was not an excellent version for its hearers? Are we not wiser to give up hankering for productions of past times until we are prepared to bring to them the minds and imaginations of past times, contenting ourselves in the twentieth century with the best that the twentieth century can do? Great plays are not bound to a single time in history, or a single group of playgoers. Their vitality asks, not for antiquarian reconstruction, but for imaginative re-creation.

Nevertheless, when we have admitted all of this we must confess that Greek plays present special problems to modern players and playgoers because they were conceived in terms very different from those which we usually associate with the theatre, and ways must be found to make them comprehensible to us.

RELIGIOUS AND MYTHICAL BACKGROUND

THE PLOTS of Greek tragedies were drawn from a body of myth and legend, more or less sacred in character, with which Greek audiences were familiar. Our situation would resemble theirs if the plots of all our plays of major importance were drawn from the Bible, and if a knowledge of the Bible might be presumed in a modern audience. (It is a curious fact, by the way, that no play of first-rate quality on a Biblical theme is to be found among the international drama of the Christian world.) This religious atmosphere did not impose any special solemnity on the Greek theatre, nor did it inhibit free criticism, but it gave the Greek playgoer a sense of taking part in a solemn and important event which is comparable in our theatre only with the spirit which is felt at a performance, for instance, of *Parsifal*. Obviously one of the first difficulties of presenting a Greek play to a modern audience is that the audience must be made acquainted, by some means or other, with the legendary background to the action which is often involved; and the audience must be persuaded, so far as possible, to take seriously forms of menace which are unfamiliar, and arbitrary actions on the part of gods in whom the spectators do not believe.

Greek plays may seem bare and strange to the playgoer who knows little about them. There are never more than three actors upon the stage at any time. The women lack charm. The action seems to proceed in jerks. The Chorus is interesting when it offers illuminating comment on the action, but much of the time it seems an intrusive nuisance. And it is impossible to persuade anyone who is truly steeped in the glories of our Elizabethan-Jacobean drama that these Greek plays are not poorer in their understanding and representation of humanity in its greatest moments. The famed Greek poetry is approached by most of us through the unsatisfactory medium of a translation, and we are informed by Greek scholars that, at its best, this dramatic poetry is inferior to Homer.

Further, there is a way of performing Greek plays, which most playgoers know, and which Stephen Leacock has aptly satirized in his own Greek play *Oroastus*; it is to be seen in those productions in which the hand of a professor of Greek is too plainly to be discerned, and in which no theatrically skilled hand appears at all. Such unfortunate ventures usually have one virtue, however; they recognize that the approach to Greek tragedy must be through formal and ritualistic playing, and that any attempts to humanize these characters or these plots is doomed to failure. The plays are about beings vastly more than life-size; and sophomoric strainings after grandiosity, painful though they may be, are greatly to be preferred to anything which cuts the Tragic Hero down to the size of that economic and political nonesuch, The Common Man.

Greek drama, then, suffers from the unfamiliarity

of its religious and legendary background, and from well-meant but theatrically unsophisticated attempts to perform it. Yet it remains one of the great dramas of the world, and from time to time finely imaginative and sensitive productions of Greek plays make it plain to us why this is so. The Stratford *Oedipus Rex* was a lightning-flash in which we saw, for an instant, this greatness revealed.

A PERFECT PLOT

WHAT ARE the qualities in *Oedipus Rex* which make it one of the mountain peaks in the world's literature? It has gripped the imagination of mankind for more than two thousand years, and during the Middle Ages, when non-Christian legends were little heeded, the story of Oedipus was considered sufficiently horrifying to be worth borrowing as a foundation for the apocryphal history of Judas. It has drawn the most extravagant praise from critics, both for its tragic grandeur and for the perfection of its plot. What is the story of the play?

Briefly, it is this: the city of Thebes suffers under a plague, and the citizens appeal to their adored king, Oedipus, for help. Who was Oedipus? Many years before the play begins, Thebes was ruled by King Laius and his Queen, Jocasta, and in their time a Sphinx appeared in the city who asked riddles of the citizens, and put them to death when they could not answer. Laius went to the Oracle at Delphi to ask for help, and was mysteriously slain while on that journey. Soon afterward a young Prince of Corinth, named Oedipus, appeared in Thebes, read the riddle of the Sphinx, and thereby drove the monster to kill herself. In gratitude the Thebans offered him their vacant throne, and Jocasta to be his bride.

When his people beg him for help Oedipus tells

113

them that he has sent his brother-in-law, Creon, to Delphi, to ask advice of the Oracle; when Creon returns he tells Oedipus that the plague is a punishment from the gods because Thebes harbours an unclean thing. The prophet Tiresias, driven by the taunts of Oedipus, tells the king that he is himself the unclean thing which the gods hate. Thereupon Oedipus searches for the truth about his own parentage and learns that he has, without knowing it, murdered his father Laius and married his mother Jocasta, and is thus irredeemably defiled. Jocasta commits suicide, Oedipus blinds himself and quits Thebes, and Creon is left to rule in his place.

WHERE DOES ITS POWER LIE?

WE MUST NOT be so foolish as to judge any play on a bare recital of its plot; *Hamlet* does not condense any more impressively than *Oedipus*. But, when we have studied the play it still appears, superficially, to be little more than another tale of the sport of the gods with man. When the prophet Tiresias tells Oedipus that he is himself the unclean thing which brings disaster upon Thebes, we believe him though Oedipus does not. We have solved the mystery of his birth long before he appears to have any hint of it. The plot which Coleridge so much admired seems to our generation, suckled on mystery stories, to be powerful but elementary. Obviously the continuing greatness of *Oedipus* must be sought elsewhere than in its plot, which we regard with respect but without wonder.

There are several good English translations of the play, but none which towers above the others, and so we cannot say that it is the poetry which holds us. Is it, then, the wisdom which Sophocles has revealed in this tragedy, the ideas expressed incidentally to the plot, which make it great? We comb the play

114

earnestly, but we find nothing uncommon in the way of wisdom. The final chorus tells us that we must consider no man happy until he is dead, which sounds like the easy gloom of first-year university students taking a survey course in philosophy.

Yet the power of the play is unquestionable, and when it is finely performed it works its magic upon us much as we suppose it did upon its first hearers in— was it 430 B.C.? It is superbly dramatic, and it strikes deep into the heart. And still we ask, Why?

THE FREUDIAN ANSWER

THE MOST convincing answer, to my mind, comes not from the realm of literary criticism but from the modern art of psycho-analysis. Perhaps the two, in their finer and truer flights, are more akin than is usually supposed. For psycho-analysis, after all, is an attempt to control and to assist, by means which are as scientific as possible, those insights into the depths of the human mind which great artists and gifted critics have always achieved in the supreme moments of their enlightenment. Whether psycho-analysis really possesses a technique of such completeness that it would enable a person of humdrum mind to discover secrets not equally visible to a person of acute intellect who did not possess the technique, is not a subject for discussion here. Perhaps it is enough to say that the great advances in the application of psycho-analysis to literature have been made by people who, apart from their psycho-analytic training, were obviously literary critics of unusual capability. Or, in other words, psycho-analysis may refine the wisdom of those who have it, but it cannot impart wisdom to those who have it not.

The problem of Oedipus lies at the root of psycho-analytic thinking, for Dr. Sigmund Freud maintained, and brought an impressive weight of clinical evidence to support his contention, that the crime of Oedipus is the crime which every man desires in his inmost heart. The infant in the cradle longs passionately to get rid of his father and be all in all to his mother; as infancy gives place to childhood this desire is thrust down into the almost inaccessible depths of the mind, but its power, and the guilt which it engenders, is a potent element in the structure of the mature mind. Writing of this play in 1897, when the concept of what is now widely known (and widely misunderstood) as the Oedipus Complex, was forming itself in his mind, Sigmund Freud wrote in a letter to a friend:

> I have found love of the mother and jealousy of the father . . . and now believe it to be a general phenomenon of early childhood . . . If that is the case, the gripping power of *Oedipus Rex*, in spite of all the rational objections to the inexorable fate that the story presupposes, becomes intelligible, and one can understand why later fate dramas were such failures. Our feelings rise against any arbitrary, individual fate such as shown in the *Ahnfrau* [a play by Grillparzer] but the Greek myth seizes on a compulsion which everyone recognizes because he has felt traces of it in himself. Every member of the audience was once a budding Oedipus in phantasy, and this dream-fulfilment played out in reality causes everyone to recoil in horror, with the full measure of repression which separates his infantile from his present state.

If we accept this hypothesis—and I hope that no reader will reject it simply on the basis of the very brief statement of it which is all that is possible in an essay of this nature—we know the secret of the immense power of *Oedipus Rex* to move audiences of widely different people: every man recognizes in Oedipus an element of himself. Of course, in all great drama we are able to identify ourselves with some of the characters, and recognize ourselves, and all human-

116

ity, in them. Nor does the psycho-analytic concept diminish the greatness of Sophocles as a playwright; he did not invent the *Oedipus* plot, but he gave it a noble form. It takes more than a dramatized exposition of a psycho-analytic idea to make a great play, or even a good one, as countless playwrights have shown.

THE SUCCESSFUL CRIMINAL

BUT THERE IS an element in Sophocles' play which I have not seen mentioned in this connection, which I believe to be important: Oedipus commits the repellent, yet desired, crime—he kills his father and possesses his mother: but—and this is vital—he *succeeds* in it. True, he blinds himself, reproaches himself at length, and tells his daughters somewhat gratuitously that his crime has blighted their lives, but he does not die, as we might expect a tragic hero to do. No, it is Queen Jocasta who dies, who finds life utterly intolerable. If it is true that Oedipus commits the crime that all men desire, and all men condemn, we may say that he pays a fairly modest price for it. Sophocles tells us of the last days of his hero in a later play, *Oedipus at Colonus*; the blinded king has had some twenty years of wandering, and though he refers to himself as an outcast, considerable honour is still paid to him; and when at last he quits this earth he does not die, but is carried away by the gods.

Is this not a surprising fate for the man that all men are said to condemn? Are we not just in saying that Oedipus does what all men desire to do, and succeeds in escaping the punishment, if not the judgment, of mankind? And if we identify ourselves with Oedipus in the play, do we not escape punishment with him? Surely some at least of the power of this play lies in a crime successfully committed, and punishment successfully escaped? Looked at in this way, we have a better understanding of the exhilaration which we feel after a successful performance of this tragedy. Oedipus kills his father, possesses his mother—and lives; tragic heroes have died by their own hand for crimes that were trivial in comparison, and we have nodded our heads and agreed that it should be so. We are content that Oedipus should pay, as it were, a heavy fine in the coin of guilt and self-reproach, which is the currency we ourselves use in expiating the same crime; it is a fate not incompatible with a large measure of happiness.

REASON A REGULATOR OF PASSION

But even those who accept the Freudian explanation, or are willing to reserve judgment on it, sometimes express surprise at the behaviour of Oedipus; he is supposed to be a man of unusual abilities, yet he is passionate and headstrong, and rushes blindly toward his fate. About this we can only say that the Greeks admired men of passion quite as much as they admired philosophers, and they were free of our modern Western delusion that reason is the measure and mainspring of action. As Bertrand Russell puts it: 'Desires, emotions, passions are the only possible causes of action; reason is not the cause of action but only a regulator.' History and personal experience do not lack for examples of men who have rushed obstinately into courses of action which reason would have forbidden. Oedipus is presented to us as a great man, not as a perfect or model man.

A QUESTION OF TRANSLATION

How did the Stratford production meet the challenges which, as we have seen, are inherent in any attempt to put this mighty play on the stage? The translation used was that of William Butler Yeats, a

118

great poet. But we may question whether his translation is a good one for a production on a large scale.

In the Yeats translation the dialogue is rendered in a dignified, but bare, prose, and the choruses are poems of great beauty and grandeur. But the prose is too close-packed to be spoken, or understood, with ease. This is a common fault of poetry rendered in another language as prose; great poetry is itself packed with meaning and allusion, for it is these qualities which make it great; to render it in prose is to produce an effect that is hard and knotted, and which has no grace of rhythm, no wings, to bear it aloft and help us to understand it. There are passages in Yeats' translation of Oedipus which sound more like translations of Tacitus.

Greek verse was poetic in every sense; not only was there elevation of thought, but there was also elevated beauty of language and every grace of rhythm and measure. These things cannot be communicated in a prose translation. It is true that some translations of this and other Greek plays have been rendered in an intolerable poetese, hard to understand, and objectionable as verse. But we need not conclude therefore that Yeats' solution is the only possible solution. Poetry must be translated into poetry if it is not to lose immeasurably in the process. Great poets rarely have the scholarship, and the quality of self-effacement, which must exist in a first-rate translator.

A COMPARISON OF TRANSLATIONS

YEATS' TRANSLATION might better be called Yeats' *version* of Oedipus. He has brought the dialogue down to good, but not fine, prose, and he has rendered parts of the choruses into verse of great beauty. This point can best be made by demonstration, and I should like here to present the reader with three versions of the

119

first chorus in the play. The first is a prose translation by Sir Richard Jebb, and we may accept it as a scholar's rendering of what the Greek verse actually says:

STROPHE I

O sweetly-speaking message of Zeus, in what spirit hast thou come from golden Pytho unto glorious Thebes? I am on the rack, terror shakes my soul, O thou Delian healer to whom wild cries rise, in holy fear of thee, what thing thou wilt work for me, perchance unknown before, perchance renewed with the revolving years: tell me, thou immortal Voice, born of Golden Hope!

ANTISTROPHE I

First call I on thee, daughter of Zeus, divine Athena, and on thy sister, guardian of our land, Artemis, who sits on her throne of fame, above the circle of our Agora, and on Phoebus the far-darter: O shine forth on me, my three-fold help against death! If ever aforetime, in arrest of ruin hurrying on the city, ye drove a fiery pest beyond our borders, come now also!

STROPHE 2

Woe is me, countless are the sorrows that I bear; a plague is on all our host, and thought can find no weapon for defence. The fruits of the glorious earth grow not; by no birth of children do women surmount the pangs in which they shriek; and life on life mayest thou see sped, like bird on nimble wing, aye, swifter than resistless fire, to the shore of the western god.

ANTISTROPHE 2

By such deaths, past numbering, the city perishes: un-pitied, her children lie on the ground, spreading pesti-lence, with none to mourn: and meanwhile young wives, and grey-haired mothers with them, uplift a wail at the steps of the altars, some here, some there, entreating for their weary woes. The prayer to the Healer rings clear, and, blent therewith, the voice of lamentation: for these things, golden daughter of Zeus, send us the bright face of comfort.

120

And grant that the fierce god of death, who now with no brazen shields, yet amid cries as of battle, wraps me in the flame of his onset, may turn his back in speedy flight from our land, borne by a fair wind to the great deep of Amphitrite, or to those waters in which none find haven, even to the Thracian wave; for if night leave aught undone, day follows to accomplish this. O thou who wieldest the powers of the fire-fraught lightning, O Zeus our father, slay him beneath thy thunderbolt!

ANTISTROPHE 3

Lycean King, fain were I that thy shafts also, from thy bent bow's string of woven gold, should go abroad in their might, our champions in the face of the foe; yea, and the flashing fires of Artemis wherewith she glances through the Lycian hills. And I call him whose locks are bound with gold, who is named with the name of this land, ruddy Bacchus to whom Bacchants cry, the comrade of the Maenads, to draw near with the blaze of his blithe torch, our ally against the god unhonoured among gods.

Thus Sir Richard Jebb. Nobody, we may safely say, would want to hear a Greek chorus talking in that strain for long. The use of archaisms and poeticisms we must allow, for Greek dramatic poets wrote in a very high-flown Greek, and not in the Greek of common speech. But we may say that this literal rendering is not poetry. How are we to get the poetry, and thus feel something of what Sophocles meant us to feel, instead of merely hearing the blunted reality of what he said? Obviously we need a poet.

A poet of no minor gifts has devoted much of his life to translating Greek drama. Gilbert Murray has translated *Oedipus Rex* into English verse, and his translation has proved itself on the stage, for it has the immense virtue of speaking well. Of his scholarship there can be no question. This is what he makes of the chorus given above:

A Voice, a Voice, that is borne on the Holy Way!
What art thou, O Heavenly One, O Word of the Houses of
Gold?
Thebes is bright with thee, and my heart leapeth; yet is it
cold,
And my spirit faints as I pray.
I-ê! I-ê!
What task, O Affrighter of Evil, what task shall thy people
essay?
One new as our new-come affliction,
Or an old toil returned with the years?
Unveil thee, thou dread benediction,
Hope's daughter and Fear's.

Zeus-Child that knowest not death, to thee I pray,
O Pallas; next to thy Sister, who calleth Thebes her own,
Artemis, named of Fair Voices, who sitteth her orbed throne
In the throng of the market way:
I-ê! I-ê!
Apollo, the Pure, the Far-smiter; O Three that keep evil
away,
If of old for our city's desire,
When the death-cloud hung close to her brow,
Ye have banished the wound and the fire,
Oh! come to us now!

Wounds beyond telling; my people sick unto death;
And where is the counsellor, where is the sword of thought?
And Holy Earth in her increase perisheth:
The child dies and the mother awaketh not.
I-ê! I-ê!
We have seen them, one on another, gone as a bird is gone,
Souls that are flame; yea, higher,
Swifter they pass than fire,
To the rocks of the dying Sun.
Their city wasteth unnumbered; their children lie
Where death hath cast them, unpitied, unwept upon.
The altars stand, as in seas of storm a high
Rock standeth, and wives and mothers grey thereon
Weep, weep and pray.
Lo, joy-cries to fright the Destroyer; a flash in the dark they
rise,

Then die by the sobs overladen.
Send help, O heaven-born Maiden,
    Let us look in the light of her eyes!

And Ares, the abhorred
    Slayer, who bears no sword,
But shrieking, wrapped in fire, stands over me,
    Make that he turn, yea, fly
    Broken, wind-wasted, high
Down the vexed hollow of the Vaster Sea;
    Or back in his own Thrace,
    To harbour shelterless.
Where Night hath spared, he bringeth end by day.
    Him, Him, O thou whose hand
    Beareth the lightning brand,
O Father Zeus, now with thy thunder, slay and slay!

    Where is thy gold-strung bow,
    O Wolf-god, where the flow
Of living shafts unconquered, from all ills
    Our helpers? Where the white
    Spears of thy Sister's light,
Far-flashing as she walks the wolf-wild hills?
    And thou, O Golden-crown,
    Theban and named our own,
O Wine-gleam, Voice of Joy, for ever more
    Ringed with thy Maenads white,
    Bacchus, draw near and smite,
Smite with thy glad-eyed flame the God whom Gods abhor.

Fault is found with Murray's translation by people
who do not like the Swinburnean opulence of his
verse. Scholars have complained that he departs from
the sense of the Greek. Yet in this instance we can see
plainly that he has given a translation of *all* that is in
the original, and if we cannot always relate his phrases
easily to the Jebb translation, we must remember that
he is translating Sophocles, and not versifying Jebb.
    This is Yeats' rendering of this same chorus:

What message comes to famous Thebes from the Golden
House?
What message of disaster from that sweet-throated Zeus?
What monstrous thing our fathers saw do the seasons bring?
Or what that no man ever saw, what new monstrous thing?
Trembling in every limb I raise my loud importunate cry,
And in a sacred terror wait the Delian God's reply.

Apollo chase the God of Death that leads no shouting men,
Bears no rattling shield and yet consumes this form with pain.
Famine takes what the plague spares, and all the crops are
lost;
No new life fills the empty place—ghost flits after ghost
To that God-ridden western shore, as flit benighted birds.
Sorrow speaks to sorrow, but no comfort finds in words.

Hurry him from the land of Thebes with a fair wind behind
Out on to that formless deep where not a man can find
Hold for an anchor-fluke, for all this world-enfolding sea;
Master of the thunder-cloud, set the lightning free,
And add the thunder-stone to that and fling them on his
head,
For death is all the fashion now, till even Death be dead.

We call against the pallid face of this God-hatred God
The springing heel of Artemis in the hunting sandal shod,
The tousle-headed Maenads, blown torch and drunken sound,
The stately Lysian king himself with golden fillet crowned,
And in his hands the golden bow and the stretched golden
string,
And Bacchus' wine-ensanguined face that all the Maenads
sing.

The merits of this are obvious. But we may see that
it is at a greater distance from Sophocles than is
Murray. And in other choruses some passages are
simply omitted. There is about Yeats' version a feeling
of compression and condensation which suggests that
it was made with some thought of performance under

those very simple and limited circumstances which Yeats so much admired. The effect is fine, in its way, but it is farther from Sophocles than is necessary in a theatre such as the one at Stratford, which is not cramped in space or pinched for money to pay actors or mount a great play greatly.

None of this, be it understood, is written in derogation of Yeats' version of *Oedipus*, so far as it goes. But it does not go far enough to give us a fully satisfactory idea of the grandeur of the original. There appears to be a notion abroad among theatre people, at present, that the Yeats' *Oedipus* is the best version for their purpose. A long look at Murray's version might change their minds.

THE FINAL CHORUS

NOT TO LABOUR the matter, but to produce a little more evidence, let us look at the brief last chorus, in which Sophocles brings out his bit of gloom, which has impressed so many people who equate gloom with wisdom. Here is Jebb's literal rendering:

> Dwellers in our native Thebes, behold, this is Oedipus, who knew the famed riddle, and was a man most mighty: on whose fortunes what citizen did not gaze with envy? Behold into what a stormy sea of dread trouble he hath come!

> Therefore, while our eyes wait to see the final destined day, we must call no one happy who is of mortal race, until he hath crossed life's border, free from pain.

Yeats boils this down to:

> Make way for Oedipus. All people said,
> 'That is a fortunate man';
> And now what storms are beating on his head!
> Call no man fortunate that is not dead.
> The dead are free from pain.

Murray, as usual more faithful and more mellifluous, has it thus:

> Ye citizens of Thebes, behold; 'tis Oedipus that
> passeth here,
> Who read the riddle-word of Death, and mightiest
> stood of mortal men,
> And Fortune loved him, and the folk that saw
> him turned and looked again.
> Lo, he is fallen, and around great storms and the
> outreaching sea!
> Therefore, O Man, beware, and look toward the
> end of things that be,
> The last of sights, the last of days; and no man's
> life account as gain
> Ere the full tale be finished and the darkness find
> him without pain.

Austerity in poetry is much admired in our day. But the language of Greek drama is not austere; it is magnificent, and that is an attribute that our age does not understand nearly so well. It may be said of Yeats' translation of this chorus that it is not only compressed, but that it is stark in a way that is untrue to the original, and that the pity for the tragic predicament of mankind which Sophocles expresses is not suggested by it. There is a blunt and minatory note in Yeats that is his own, not Sophocles' and he ends the tragedy not with a dying fall, but with the slamming of a door.

PERSONALITY AT A MINIMUM

IN THE STRATFORD PRODUCTION of *Oedipus* Dr. Guthrie and Miss Moiseiwitsch used several interesting expedients to present the play as ritual, with the least possible intrusion of human personality. Although the costumes derived from Greek models, limbs and flesh were not

ELEANOR STUART
as
JOCASTA
and as herself

seen; the players wore masks which prevented any play of feature; the principal actors wore boots with soles several inches thick, like the Greek cothurnus, which imposed upon them the stately walk of the Greek tragic stage. These appurtenances gave them almost an extra foot in height. Thus they appeared to us as beings of a greater consequence than the Chorus, who wore masks only, and the Chorus in their turn were greater than the Suppliants, whose masks were meagre and had little stamp of character. 'Tragedy concerneth a high fellow,' said Sir Philip Sidney, and in this production we were left in no doubt as to who were high fellows and who were underlings.

This was in the true spirit of Greek tragedy, which exaggerates the distinctions between man and man to a degree which now requires some explanation to an audience. In *Hamlet* we know that the Prince and the Grave Digger are different in spirit, but not in kind; in modern drama the distinctions between man and man are dealt with so gingerly that tragedy in the classical sense is almost impossible; in Greek drama the difference between Oedipus and the Suppliants is that between a creature who is the nearest thing to a god on earth, and a slave who is little above a beast of burden. Only in Greek Comedy do the lower orders of mankind have individuality, or much to say for themselves. In the Stratford *Oedipus* this distinction was made visible, and in this fact lay one of the great virtues of the production. In performances of this play without masks the distinction between the relative importance of one character and another in the eyes of the gods—which is very much the same thing as the eyes of the audience—can never be as striking as it is when masks are used.

THE STRATFORD MASKS were splendid creations. They were, in reality, casts taken from clay models, in gauze and *papier mâché,* covered with chamois; but as they appeared to the playgoer the face of Oedipus was a superb, sun-like visage of gold, from which the pinnacles of his crown branched out like the rays of the Sun himself. Jocasta's mask was a Moon to this Sun, and it might have been said that this Moon was severer in expression than is usual in representations of the Queen of Heaven. The face of Creon was of a dark bronze, withdrawn and watchful. These three royal persons, with their great metallic heads, were obviously the most important characters in the drama, and the grandeur of their robes completed a magnificence which no unmasked actor could hope to attain.

Apart from these, the most striking figure in the play was the blind prophet Tiresias, whose mask suggested the bony head of a bird, ivory-white, beaked and sightless. The Man from Corinth wore a bucolic mask, broad and good-natured, and the Old Shepherd might almost have been one of his sheep, woolly, humble and submissive. The Messenger's mask, though grave, was not marked by woe; this was the face of Sober Report.

But while all these masks were finely conceived and admirably expressive of character, it was in the masks for the fifteen Theban Elders who comprised the Chorus that the art of the designers and makers was most impressively displayed. Though all bore a family resemblance, all were individually characterized, and each one was so well suited to the wearer that those in the audience who knew the actors in the Chorus were quickly able to identify them. While such identification was not necessary and may not even have been desirable, it was an astonishing feat to have given something of the wearer's identity to each one. These fifteen faces, gnarled with age and wisdom, marked sometimes by the minor deformities of years, were wonderful presentations of understanding, compassion and resignation. Here, as with the principal characters, we were given masks which were abstracts of humanity, rather than humanity itself; in these faces we saw the wisdom and beauty of age, purged of weakness or triviality.

It would be foolishly dogmatic to say that Greek tragedy should not be played except in masks. Two great performances of *Oedipus* have already been mentioned in this essay, in which masks were not used, and doubtless we shall see others. But undeniably the use of masks gives a magnificence, an aloof grandeur, when the masks are finely conceived and made, that is not within the range of any human face. It is such magnificence as the Greek theatre prized, and the Stratford audiences were privileged to see a Greek convention splendidly adapted to the theatre of our day. There was nothing tricky, nothing self-conscious, about this use of masks; it was part of a great conception, and could not have been spared without diminishing the whole.

RITUAL AND CHOREOGRAPHY

As with the masks, so was it also with the ritual approach to the action of the drama. Ritual is a means of evoking something too great for realistic presentation. If we accept the Freudian interpretation of the plot of *Oedipus*, the play is a ritual which dredges up from the depths of memory a primary experience of mankind, which is normally repressed. Plays of incest do not strike us dumb, and leave us elevated as does

ROBERT GOODIER
as
CREON
and as himself

Oedipus, unless they plunge very deep into the wells of the spirit; the mere presentation of incest on the stage or in a novel may leave us unmoved or, worse still, it may provoke cynical laughter. But the hold which *Oedipus* has upon us is the hold of truth itself. Great truths are best presented by symbols, and by ritual, as all the great faiths of the world have shown.

The movement of the actors in this production was slow, hieratic and more like dancing than we are used to seeing even on the classical stage. The movement was not dictated by the obvious necessities of the plot so much as it was in itself a support and an amplification of what was being said, and of what was happening in the minds of the characters. It was in this production that Tyrone Guthrie's idea of 'choreography' in drama was triumphantly demonstrated. In the Greek theatre dancing was a vital part of the performance and at Stratford we saw in the ritual of the performance, as well as in the masks, the spirit of the Greek theatre given a modern dwelling; this was not antiquarianism, but re-creation.

The matter of the translation used in this production has already been discussed, but we must return to it briefly in order to make a general comment on the acting. When we go to see *Oedipus Rex* we have a right to expect acting and declamation on the fullest classical scale. But the actor who is faced with the sober and occasionally commonplace rhythms of the prose which Yeats has used for the dialogue in this version of the play must suit his declamation to the matter that is given him; when he has spoken clearly and intelligibly, he has done all that he is called upon to do; there is no poetry to challenge him, or to carry him on its wings. To this playgoer, at least, there was a laconic quality about the dialogue which robbed

132

DONALD DAVIS
as
TIRESIAS
and as himself

the tragedy of its full effect; where we expected the grandeur of poetry we heard the terse prose of a good lecture. Yet there were actors at Stratford who would have seized upon poetry eagerly, and who could have delighted and shaken us with it.

THE TRAGIC HERO

First in the cast we must consider James Mason, who played the central role of Oedipus. He brought to it a nobility of bearing, and a fine certainty and repose which enabled him to hold long pauses, and to fill them with meaning. When we remember that this was done while wearing a mask which concealed any play of expression, we can be in no doubt of the actor's mastery of his part. There were no superfluous gestures—nothing but deliberate movements of head and hands, and expressive speech.

Much—perhaps too much—was made of the lightness and limited range of this actor's voice. Certainly a player of tragic roles is fortunate if he has a voice with a beautiful and individual tone, great power, and a big range. But it is not absolutely necessary that he should have such a voice and more than one tragic actor of the first order has lacked this gift. We need only mention the name of Henry Irving to make this clear. James Mason's voice is a light baritone which he produces in a deliberate and somewhat dry manner which robs it of sonority, though not of music. He has his own way of making his effects, and it is a deeply telling way. Who that heard it can forget the cry of pain which Laurence Olivier gave when, as Oedipus, the full horror of his fate broke upon him? It was an animal roar which seemed to come from his whole body, and not from his mouth alone; it struck terror to the heart. But, in the same place, James Mason gave

134

a cry of a very different sort, a cry on a descending cadence, which pierced the heart with pity. In the context of this production it was no less true, no less moving. To have produced such a cry as Olivier's, in proper proportion, from within the costume and mask which Mason wore would have demanded the lungs of Stentor. The actor was entirely right to seek his effect in a different way. It is not simply the voice, but the art and the mind controlling the voice, which gives truth to a performance.

A fine artistic truth informed James Mason's performance of Oedipus at all times. The play is not subtle, but monumental, and the descent from the superb pride of Oedipus to his final mutilation and self-loathing is steep and uninterrupted. The actor gave us what the play and the production called for, and at the end of the first performance he won a heartfelt and tumultuous ovation from the audience, who stood to cheer him. As the festival went on, his performance grew until, when last he gave it, it had risen to a memorable tragic level. It was the unquestioned crown of the finest production of the 1954 festival.

IN THE SHADOW OF THE HERO

THE GREEK CONCEPT of the Tragic Hero does not allow of roles which are in any sense of comparable importance in the same play. But *Oedipus Rex* contains several parts which demand notable qualities of the actors, for, with the exception of Jocasta and Creon, they must make their full effect within the limits of a single scene. At Stratford, the impersonality of the production, and especially the masks, imposed upon the actors a greater degree of anonymity than is usual. They were like a team of bell-ringers, each

135

DOUGLAS CAMPBELL
as the MAN FROM CORINTH

WILLIAM NEEDLES
as the OLD SHEPHERD

DOUGLAS RAIN
as the MESSENGER

ERIC HOUSE
as the PRIEST

with one note to sound loud and clear, but no extended range. If the comments on the performances which follow seem brief, it is because of this fact, and not from any unwillingness to give the players their due.

Jocasta was played by Miss Eleanor Stuart; she gave the role nobility and strength, but we would have welcomed more suggestion of the Desired and Feared Mother. Jocasta may not make a sentimental appeal to the audience, but the full horror of the tragedy can only be achieved if we feel that she and her son brought passionate appetite to their ill-fated mating. In her performance of this part Miss Stuart was ill-served by her mask and costume, which were in shades of silver, suggesting a coldness which was hostile to her appearance as a beloved wife. Her mask, in particular, was moulded in chilling and minatory lines which suggested a Victorian governess rather than the mother whom every man desires in his heart. The actress spoke finely and moved with grace, but in a production where costume and mask were of such importance she was unable to overcome errors which were not of her making.

As Creon, Robert Goodier was well served by his fine voice, and the bronze mask which he wore was watchful, sardonic and detached, as Creon must be if we remember the part which he plays later in the history of the children of Oedipus. Creon has two splendid moments, first when he denies the accusation of treachery which Oedipus makes against him, and second, when he adjures the self-deposed king not to seek to be master in Thebes; the actor rose fittingly to both of these climaxes.

Even Sophocles, conscious as he was of the supremacy of the Tragic Hero, was not immune from a difficulty which afflicts all authors—the difficulty of

138

the minor character who threatens to eclipse the major one. Shakespeare had to kill Mercutio to keep him from taking the play away from Romeo: Sophocles removes the prophet Tiresias from the stage just in time to keep him from overwhelming Oedipus. In the Stratford production the blind seer appeared in the extreme of physical infirmity, without the usual boy to guide him (mentioned in the text, but for some reason dispensed with) and limping hideously; at one alarming moment he fell headlong down a flight of steps into the arms of the Chorus, and at another he pursued the king about the stage, hopelessly lost. The contrast between the light of truth within him and the darkness in which he moved was hammered home with cruel, telling blows. Donald Davis, who played this part, has a large voice, dark in tone and of great range. He made of the blind prophet a character second only to the tragic king himself, and brought a terror to the performance which seemed to spring from the remotest deeps of the mind, where primal terrors dwell.

We do not expect any lightening of the darkness in this tragedy, but Douglas Campbell contrived to bring some sunlight into it with a striking conception of the Man from Corinth. This fellow from Corinth is not a particularly pleasant character; he brings news of the death of the supposed father of Oedipus, hoping to get a reward. But the actor made him an engaging, guileless yokel, whose free admission of his purpose brought the single laugh of the production. Some auditors thought that the cadence with which he spoke suggested the Highlands of Scotland; others were equally determined that it was Welsh; it was unquestionably rural, and it had a convincing ring of a shepherd about it, and that was sufficient. The other rustic, the Old Shepherd, was played by William

Needles with touching humility and resignation. The small part of the Priest of Zeus was played by Eric House, who gave, in his few speeches, the sense of the anguish of the plague-stricken city without which the play cannot begin in the proper key.

In a Greek play the role of the Messenger is of special significance, for it was not the Greek custom to show the climax of the action before the audience; the culminating horror of the tragedy was always described, in a speech of great power. Douglas Rain was the Messenger who told the shuddering Elders of Thebes of the death of Jocasta, and of the grief and self-mutilation of Oedipus. This actor has an excellent voice and great emotional power, and in his single great scene he produced precisely the effect of mounting horror which the tragedy calls for. When Oedipus, uncrowned, robed in crimson and with his head shrouded in a veil, appeared from the door of the palace, the audience had been brought to a pitch of excitement and anticipation worthy of that great moment; this was the purgation through pity and terror of which Aristotle wrote, and which he insisted upon as the true effect of great tragedy. No Greek tragedy can make its full effect without an actor of great abilities to play its Messenger, and Stratford was memorably served in this respect.

THE CHORUS

THE CHORUS of Theban Elders, led by William Hutt, was admirable and one is tempted to say that it was, collectively, the best actor in the play. The choruses were spoken, and these fifteen men brought passion and compassion to them in a measure which, time and again, moved the hearer as only great poetry, greatly spoken, can move him. It was when the Chorus spoke that we felt the indescribable but unmistakable thrill which we wanted in the dialogue of the actors, but which the prose version could not give us. This was not 'verse speaking', good though that may be. It was certainly not a 'speech choir'—that device by which many speakers are used to produce less effect than one good speaker. It was the collective voice of age and wisdom, as Sophocles meant it to be. We forgave them for not singing, as a Greek Chorus should, they spoke so well. We forgave them—until, magically, they broke into song in a simple, but beautiful and eloquent setting of the invocation to Mount Cithaeron. Then we regretted deeply the fact that all the choruses had not been given suitable music by Cedric Thorpe Davie. This is not to wish that *Oedipus* had been turned into an opera; it was, rather, to wish that the Stratford actors had mastered the Habima Players' way of moving easily from speech into song, when song heightens without interrupting the drama. It was —to repeat a criticism by now familiar in this essay— to wish that what we heard as prose had been renderd as poetry, and that what was given as poetry had been delivered as song. For the full poetic and human truth of *Oedipus Rex* cannot be fully achieved in any other way. Poetry and song would have completed the nobly ritual effect which was so finely achieved in the appearance of the production.

But it is not the purpose of this book to grieve for what was not, but to celebrate, as justly as possible, what was accomplished. This was a production of a great tragedy which achieved its full effect within the limitations which it had set upon itself; it was a production which gave us, again and again, the mingled terror and delight of self-recognition, which this tragedy is particularly able to evoke. It carried Canadian actors and Canadian audiences into new territory which, now seized, must not be relinquished.

141

A LONG VIEW OF THE STRATFORD FESTIVAL

By TYRONE GUTHRIE

THE STRATFORD FESTIVAL has now survived its second season. Perhaps the artistic success of the second has not quite equalled that of the first. I think in our press notices a polite suggestion of disappointment was to be detected. But then the first year had been highly praised largely because the whole thing was a surprise; people were kindly and generously applauding a daring experiment which had, in part, succeeded. The second year's performances had to be not merely as good but better than the first. Inevitably there were shortcomings, and these, justly enough, received more stringent comment than those of the first year. But, on the whole, in my opinion, the performances in the second year *were* better, inasmuch as the general level of the acting was more skilful, more assured, and more variety of talent was displayed.

In the first year, although there were only four British actors, the weight they pulled was out of all proportion to their numbers. Also the plays did not present the same opportunity for teamwork as they did in the second year. *Richard III* is essentially a 'star' piece; the rest of the parts are short and provide only momentary chances. But in *Measure for Measure* the distribution of parts is far more even, and two of the three chief characters were played by Canadian actors. In *The Taming of the Shrew* both the leading players were Canadian. In *Oedipus Rex* I thought that the Chorus—all Canadian actors—gave quite a remarkable display of technique and discipline, each actor entirely forgoing any chance to shine individually and allowing himself to become just one fifteenth

145

of a single but elaborate and exceedingly difficult con-
certed manoeuvre.

The success at the box-office was most satisfactory.
And the Governors of the Festival are now in a position
to believe that, given a reasonably prudent administration, matched with a reasonably daring artistic
policy, and a reasonable share of luck, their enterprise
may be regarded as an annual event.

This presupposes some long-term plans. In the following pages I propose to discuss some of the bases
for such plans. I have the approval of the Governors to
express my own views here, but they are not 'official',
and of course do not commit the Governors to any
course of action, or even to any corporate agreement
with the ideas here expressed.

FIRST OF ALL, the housing of the project. The Tent,
which at present provides the roof and walls of the
theatre, has enabled a drastic experiment to be made
in staging Shakespeare and in actor-audience relation,
without involving the project in crippling expense.

The Tent, however, will not last indefinitely. In less
than ten years it will have to be replaced. Already the
Governors must be starting to consider whether, and
how, to replace it. I think there is general agreement
that, when the life of the present tent comes to an
end, it should not necessarily mean the end of the
Stratford Festival. But to replace the existing tent by
another does not seem the wisest idea. Although the
initial outlay was less than it would have been on a
building of more solid type, the cost of erecting, dis-
mantling and maintaining a tent is high, and will get
higher as the tent gets older and more decrepit. Moreover the tent is not well adapted to extreme weather

146

conditions. On hot nights the audience and actors are fried in their own fat. On cold nights the play is given to a castanet *obbligato* of chattering teeth. In a high wind the gallant Tabernacle rocks and creaks like a windjammer at sea. Rain drumming on the canvas roof makes a most glorious Wagnerian effect but it completely, if temporarily, obliterates the puny competition offered by the actors. A more solid structure is clearly indicated. But of what kind?

I sincerely hope that the Governors will stick to the arena stage and wide amphitheatre. First, I consider that it has proved the point that Shakespearean plays gain enormously in impact by relating actors to audience as nearly as possible in what we can conclude to have been the relation which prevailed in Shakespeare's own time, and for which the plays were written.

Evidence on this relation is, admittedly, incomplete. But it all points to two facts: that there was no illusionary scenery, and that the actors were so near their audience that they could speak really low and still be heard; so near their audience that small shades of expression, subtle effects, could make their point. An audience large enough to make adequate productions pay their way can only be as near as this to the actors if the amphitheatre plan be adopted, because only in this way can the cubic capacity of an auditorium be used economically.

At Stratford the amphitheatre holds almost two thousand people, and the farthest seats are only sixteen rows back. Admittedly the Stratford amphitheatre has hitherto embraced rather too wide a sector; the extreme side seats have been too far around to the side of the stage. This defect is being remedied. And, in this connection, it must be remembered that this temporary amphitheatre is on one level only. There is no gallery. In a more permanent building, by providing a second tier of seats suspended above the first, it should be possible to maintain capacity at about two thousand but at the same time to use a somewhat reduced sector and to keep the farthest people no more than ten or twelve rows from the front.

If, however, the Governors do plump for an 'Elizabethan' stage and an amphitheatre, their building will not be suitable for the production of all and sundry kinds of dramatic entertainment. Nor will it be rentable as a skating rink, for dances, badminton, church teas, and other activities from which the owners of All-purpose Halls derive revenue. On the other hand it must be remembered that an All-purpose Hall can also, and I think more correctly, be regarded as a No-purpose Hall. The mind of man has yet to devise a building that will accomodate activities of every kind suitably; and in seeking to make all things possible, the All-purpose Hall is never more than a series of makeshifts and compromises. Stratford already has a City Hall and an Armoury, both of traditional and quite remarkable ugliness; but there they are, and their existence should be at once an Awful Warning, and a relief from the responsibility of having to erect yet another All-purpose Hall. In my view, then, the Governors should decide to aim at building a specifically Festival Theatre; and, since the period of the Festival would seem to be limited to something around, or a little less than, three months in the Summer, I think it should be a specifically Summer palace, soundproof, rain-proof, heat-proof, but no more adapted to contend with all seasons than with all purposes.

Without any precise idea of how it should look, I envisage a building which has the courage of this conviction: that a theatre is a Temple dedicated to the service of that God, or that aspect of One Almighty God, which is concerned with Fantasy. The one further injunction about its appearance which I would lay upon its architect would be that it should look welcoming, should look like a place where you go to enjoy yourself. Too many theatres aim to look like royal palaces. But Theatre Royal is apt to be Theatre Pompous. And anyway a royal palace nowadays is bound to be mistaken for an insurance office or a bank.

It seems to me vastly important that the idea of Art should be closely associated with that of Pleasure. Now that the private patronage of great wealth has been virtually abolished by taxation, the Muses have to go cap in hand to government officials begging for bread. The most likely government department to 'touch' is that of Education; so there is a sad tendency to put a case for support by stressing the Educational Aspect of Art.

There are two chief criteria by which the educational potentialities of a theatrical enterprise are judged. First is it likely to produce material which is 'on the Syllabus'? Funds can be given or withheld by dullards who ask whether a play will be performed because it is a Set Book, which young people are forced to swot in order to be examined in a subject called Literature.

The second criterion is more general. It is related to the question as to whether a play is, in a wide sense, 'educational'. That is, of course, more reasonable than relating it to exams. But the difficulty is: what is, or is not, educational? In general Civil Service practice, Shakespeare is educational, the Restoration Dramatists very definitely are not; Sheridan and Gold-

smith are on the borderline; foreign plays are doubtful starters—foreigners are apt to express subversive
ideas about all sorts of things; a modern play has no
chance at all. Even Shakespeare is a bit unreliable.
Most of his plays are concerned with quite un-educational ideas like adultery and murder; and even the
'nice' plays are full of un-educational words like
'whoremaster' or 'belly'. Ideas as to what constitutes
education are, most rightly, inextricably intertwined
with ideas about morality. Consequently theatrical
people have to go around pretending that their job is
to Do Good to their fellow-men, rather than to amuse
them.

I am an unashamed advocate of what dry-as-dust
pedagogues derisively term the 'Play-Way', for education, and all other activities. I contend that you really
only apprehend what you *want* to apprehend and that
the best form of education is to find means of inducing
a student to want to teach himself.

It has not been my experience that any of us really
wants anything because someone else says This Is
Good For You. By bitter experience we have all learnt
that, if people say a thing is good for you, it is merely
a ruse to induce you to undergo a thoroughly unpleasant experience. And so conditioned are we to this
proposition that, conversely and perversely, we are all
disinclined to accept a thing as good for us unless it is
also thoroughly unpleasant. No one thinks well of a
medicine which tastes nice; to be good for you it must
taste filthy and if possible smell filthy, and look filthy
too; disinfectants must *sting*; a Good Book must be
a penance to read—it's one of the reasons why the
Bible is printed as it is. If by any chance you enjoy a
piece of music or a play, you have to laugh off your
enjoyment by some derogatory phrase, 'purely frivol-

ous, of course','nothing much to it', in order to pretend that you only get Real Pleasure out of far sterner stuff.

But isn't it the case that we really only learn from experiences which touch us emotionally—either with pleasure or pain? And that the more intense the emotion the more powerfully the experience is etched on the plate of memory? That is why most of us have long forgotten the greater part of the knowledge which was painfully stuffed into us at school. Important, interesting things are clean forgotten because they were never emotionally etched upon the mind; whereas we remember absurd scraps—the population of Halifax in 1910; the specific gravity of cotton—because for some, usually irrelevant, reason such scraps are associated with an emotional experience.

For this reason the Theatre should assert its claim to be educational, not because it is a short cut to examination answers, nor because it is morally uplifting, but because it widens the imaginative horizon by presenting ideas in the most memorable way. The ideas evoked by the Theatre are, if the actors are doing their work adequately, primarily emotional. They drive consciously at the sources of pleasure and pain; and by that means produce impressions, not only far more vivid but far more lasting, than experiences which are more purely intellectual.

Therefore those who are concerned with Education do well to be wary of the influence of the Arts; and particularly the Arts of the Theatre. That must be admitted. The mistake, however, which they commonly make—I suggest this in all humility—is to apply the customary Puritan formula: What is good for you must be unpleasant; and its converse: What is pleasant therefore cannot be good for you. What is pleasant *can* be, and usually is, good for you. Nature sees to that.

151

What is bad for you is boredom, being made to undergo experiences which have for you no meaning, which do not ring your bell.

There is in this day and age a very real danger that the Theatre is divided into two directly opposed categories: first, Show Business which is fun, sexy and frivolous, educational only in the same sense as drunkeness or rape; second, the Serious Theatre, which is educational in the same sense as quadratic equations, and is a thundering, pompous, unmitigated but anæmic bore.

The first is so popular a diversion that it is able to operate profitably under what is flatteringly termed Private Enterprise. The second can only operate if it is given constant injections of public money. Well, of course commercial success is no guarantee of quality. I am all for public funds being available for the Theatre, just as they are for picture galleries, libraries, museums, universities and zoos. My objection is that before it gets public funds, the Theatre is virtually obliged to represent itself as an anæmic goody-goody bore.

If Stratford is to have a Festival Theatre it must proclaim by its very appearance that this is a Temple where levity and mirth are not excluded, but where it is recognized that levity and mirth are all part of one emotional axis at whose opposite pole lie gravity and tears; that if Jehovah is to be glorified so also is Baal to be mocked; that fun can be serious; that seriousness need not be pompous; that education can be conducted not only in cap and gown, but also, and no less effectually, in cap and bells.

I AM AWARE that the greatest single factor that has enabled the Festival to establish itself has been completely outside the control of those concerned. I refer to the fact of its timeliness. However carefully the Festival might have been organized, however brilliant the performances might have been, it would have availed nothing if there had not been a public hungry and eager for the kind of fare that was offered.

Now here I am going to venture some opinions of a general nature about a vague entity known as 'Canada', and a group of my fellow creatures loosely grouped together under the heading 'Canadians'. I am aware that it is fatally easy, and often fatally unwise, for visitors to land out with assertions based on their own early impressions of a new environment. Europeans never stop handing out information about 'America' and even advice to 'Americans', based on the evidence gathered in a week's visit to New York. And this kind of nonsense is a two-way traffic. I never stop listening to confident generalizations on the question of Irish Partition from lively visitors who have just flown in from Chicago, motored west through blinding rain to see the farm where Grandma was raised, then after lunch, not on the farm but in an hotel, have motored south through blinding rain to see Grandpa's tombstone, getting back to Dublin in time for dinner at the Shelbourne. If they are 'serious' they spend a day in Dublin 'doing' the well sign-posted Joyce relics, including some surviving Joyce relatives, after which they feel equipped to tell the world all about Ireland. It does not occur to them to visit Belfast. Belfast is 'ugly'; Belfast is obsessed with Business; Belfast people have the most ghastly accent; they are 'common'— you've only to be in Dublin five minutes to be told all that as an absolute fact. Similarly, lively visitors to Scotland from overseas spend a week at the Edinburgh Festival where they meet Gregory Peck, some delightful opera singers from New Jersey, Thornton Wilder and the Catholic Archbishop of Saint Louis. Then, after a coach trip, in blinding rain, through the Trossachs, a coach trip, in blinding rain, through the Scott Country (tea at Abbotsford), a steamer trip through the Kyles of Bute, in blinding rain, they feel—and who wouldn't?—equipped to issue press statements upon Scottish Nationalism, Scottish dialect, Scottish vigour, Scottish decadence, the economic plight of the Highlands, the future of Scottish Football and, of course, the influence of the Scottish climate.

And yet . . . and yet.

What do they know of Ireland, Scotland or even Canada, who only Ireland, Scotland, or even Canada, know? The confident generalizations of lively visitors obviously are not the whole truth. But the whole truth on such matters just is not accessible. It just is not possible to assimilate completely so large and complex a unit even as Ireland, let alone Canada. Therefore I shall not be too apologetic. I do not ask to have my generalizations accepted as The Truth; merely as impressions based upon a limited but first-hand experience.

A large number and a wide variety of Canadians are becoming more and more conscious that in many important respects Canada is a very dull place to live in; that economic opportunities are immense but, having made enough money to live comfortably, there is comparatively little in Canada to nourish the spirit. And yet the economic opportunities are making it possible for an ever-growing number of people to have a considerable amount of leisure, and are making it possible for an ever-growing number of people to be expensively and elaborately educated. They are equipped with money, leisure, and an awareness of 'culture' for which there is therefore a large demand but, as yet, a very small supply.

154

Many people are also aware that a rich Canada will be a powerful factor in world affairs, an important influence in human development. Power and influence carry responsibilities. To shoulder such responsibilities adequately Canadians will have to be more than just materially rich.

It is fairly evident that with increasing riches and comfort the pioneer vigour of body and spirit soon decays. Spiritual simplicity rarely outlives hard conditions. Peasant virtues of thrift, honesty, industry certainly can and do survive transplanting into more sophisticated conditions, but they only survive by adaptation to the new environment. Such adaptation, in broad terms, is what I believe the term culture ought to mean.

Canada, therefore, at the present moment is a 'sellers' market' for culture: the demand is greater than the supply. That is why the Stratford Festival was hailed with such enthusiasm, why it has had such striking economic success, why it has become—out of all proportion to the size of the undertaking, or its quality in relation to similar Festivals elsewhere (Salzburg, for instance, or Edinburgh)—'important', a symbol of a new spirit in Canada.

It is against this background that the Governors of the Festival must plan its future.

THE CENTRAL POINT of planning seems to me to be the choice of programme.

The first year we concentrated solely on the production of two plays. Rightly, I think. Even so we bit off almost more than we could all chew, so difficult was the job of starting from scratch. Finance was the toughest problem, since not unnaturally people were

155

chary of offering large sums to further a project which, however admirable in intention, did not look at all likely to be solvent or offer any guarantee that it would even be artistically creditable. Then there were all the building problems; then those of booking and advertising; then those of accommodation not only for a cast and staff of about a hundred, but for the nightly influx of theatre-goers—two thousand people most of whom wanted an evening meal, and about half of whom wanted bed and breakfast. In other words there was a sizable job of administration which had to be tackled by people most of whom had no previous experience of what they were undertaking; and none of whom had a really clear idea of the results expected.

On the theatrical side, there was a company to be recruited and welded into some kind of artistic and moral unity; that was comparatively easy because of the great goodwill of the actors. It was more difficult to set up a mechanism for making the costumes, properties and accessories, so that again there should be some artistic cohesion. The Professional Theatre had never had very firm roots in Canada. There had once been a fine market for visiting stars and touring companies; but resident companies had never, so far as I can gather, operated upon any considerable scale. And the Amateur Theatre, which has for the past thirty years done a fine job in keeping 'live' Theatre alive, never operated in a manner that made possible the existence of theatrical workshops and warehouses which could supply what we needed. We were in this respect like real pioneers. Most of the things we required were not to be had by sending to a store and buying them. We had to get hold of the raw material, set to and make them.

To get the theatre built, to get the plays on, and to

provide the mechanism for administering the season, fully occupied all available energies the first year. Nevertheless some of our visitors felt that if they made the pilgrimage to the plays, it would be nice if Stratford offered them a little more to do. They complained that a tour of the Railway Works, the Mausoleum, the Hospital, the Sewage Disposal Plant and the 'Y', though fascinating, was not enough. And we agreed.

So the second year we determined to extend the Festival's range of attractions. We mounted three instead of two productions. In addition there was an interesting exhibition of contemporary Canadian painting, and another of theatrical art, comparing decors and architecture in the theatres of many different epochs and parts of the world. There was also a two week's Seminar conducted by senior members of the Festival company and staff. Applications for this considerably exceeded the numbers of students who could be taken; and it should be possible to develop this branch of the Festival's activity interestingly and usefully.

Unfortunately putting on three plays in quick succession nearly broke the back of the production staff. In theory *Oedipus Rex* was to be a simple production. The cast was comparatively small. Each of the actors would wear only one dress. There were very few properties. The play was short and would require far less rehearsal than a large Shakespearean effort. That was in December 1953; in Ireland; on paper.

By March it was clear that we had made a slight underestimate of the work. Masks would be required; and if the Chorus were to be any good it would need a very great deal of rehearsal indeed. However the mask difficulty was not insurmountable; there had been a similar problem with the armour for *Richard*

157

III the year before; and the Chorus could be rehearsed, just like the fight at the end of *Richard*, for an hour every evening. No difficulty really, if one had a Sensible Plan.

What we had failed to foresee was that the effort of putting on three plays is much more than one third greater than the effort of putting on two. Had we all been fresh there would have been ample time to prepare *Oedipus*. But everyone was tired. Tired people take longer to do anything than fresh people. The effort to keep up to schedule made everyone more and more tired. Tiredness made everyone prone to colds. *Oedipus* got on only through a barrage of catarrh and by the skin of its teeth. But a lesson has been learnt. Without a much larger staff, which in present conditions would be extravagant, two productions are as much as can be prudently undertaken.

THE DRAMATIC PROGRAMME will continue to be classical. We conceive it to be the most useful function which the Stratford Festival can perform. In the first place a classical programme is the indispensable training ground both for the practitioners and connoisseurs of any art. In Canada, except at Stratford, there exists at present no other opportunity to present a classical programme on any considerable scale. There have been, and will be more, classical productions of merit but for economic, as well as artistic, reasons it is most unlikely that, except in Festival conditions, there can be productions on the scale which we have been able to present; or that, for some years, another theatre will exist in Canada with the particular intention of presenting a planned series of big classical plays.

There is in Canada a remarkable supply of gifted

158

actors. The Dominion Drama Festival, The Canadian Broadcasting Corporation, which has a particularly distinguished dramatic record, and more recently television, and a growing number of small professional theatres have given them opportunities to get experience. A young actor in Toronto at the present time has, in my opinion, a better chance to earn a living, than he would have in London or New York, where the market is grossly over-supplied and where the pressure of competition is stifling. But while in Toronto, Montreal and other Canadian centres the economic opportunity is good, the artistic opportunities are rather limited. Chances to act upon the stage before an audience are rare, the quality of stage productions, though rapidly improving, is not as yet equal to the standard in London or New York. There are lessons which can only be learnt in front of an audience, which films, radio and T.V. can never teach. For instance, one of the most important weapons in an actor's armoury is to know how to 'feel' an audience; to react to the audience's reaction. This is partly a matter of instinct, but also largely of experience. And such experience is not one of the things which a studio can supply. There are technical lessons too which radio and film acting cannot teach—notably how to declaim. The microphone is inimical to declamation. But in the theatre it is essential not merely to make oneself audible at some distance, but to have at command the full range of the voice from a whisper to a shout. Radio and film acting can often be subtle and interesting but it is always a matter of fine shades, small effects; it is as though a painter were always obliged to work on a tiny canvas with a strictly limited palette. There is no opportunity for the sweeping bold strokes, the thunderous attack, the effects of violent contrast, the large-

ciency, but they forget that there are whole ranges of ideas, whole fields of expression, of the most profound and universal significance, which never 'get into the papers', which for one reason or another are considered 'un-commercial'.

I take it that a Festival such as Stratford should assume that the large majority of its patrons are theatrically inexperienced but are not therefore unintelligent. Their judgment, if unsophisticated, will be all the fresher. If they have bothered to come some distance, and have paid quite a high price, to see a play, most of them will, I imagine, be prepared to give to it their serious critical attention. So they must not be played down to. The programme must be chosen from plays which may be held to have some significance, which have something serious to say (all great comedies are serious; seriousness and fun are not antithetical), which enshrine some universal truth to human experience.

Now judgment of contemporary plays, even by very gifted and experienced people, is constantly shown to be fallible. All too often their swans are geese. Moreover the taste of experts is apt to be far too advanced for ordinary playgoers. The only possible assurance in this matter is to choose plays which are agreed to be significant not merely by contemporary judgment but by that of good critics over a considerable period of time, work in fact which has survived the ins and outs of mere fashion and has been held in respect by several generations of critics. In other words, works which have become Classics.

Now the Festival was originated with the idea that it should be primarily a Shakespearean occasion; the theatre and stage have been designed primarily for the production of Shakespeare. They are not, in my

161

opinion, architecturally suitable for the kind of plays written for a proscenium theatre, and that includes the Classic Drama since the second half of the seventeenth century. But I hope that the policy of the Festival will not exclude all plays other than those of Shakespeare. Though the greatest, he is not the only great playwright of his epoch; and the stage is not, in my opinion, unsuitable for many kinds of drama besides the Elizabethan. It is my hope that, while Shakespeare continues to be the mainstay of the programme, other suitable and significant works may frequently be given. There are dozens which would otherwise hardly ever be produced on the American continent, and which are infinitely more illuminating and rewarding on the stage than on the shelf. In this respect we of the English-speaking world are like the possessor of the finest collection of pictures in the world. A very few of them are on the walls; a large number, of no less excellence, are kept in store and are never seen by anybody.

If the Governors were in general agreement about the merit and suitability of a new play, I greatly hope that they would back their fancy and give it a showing. It must be remembered, however, that the risk of such a step—financial and artistic—is very great. While a too cautious policy in the Theatre is a slow death by pernicious anæmia, an over-adventurous policy leads to sudden death in embarrassingly public circumstances—a fatal seizure at mid-day in the Market Place.

It may be asked, why—if the programme is to be classical—the plays hitherto chosen have not been those which are considered the greatest. Why, for example, choose such an obvious doubtful starter as *All's Well That Ends Well*, or such an obvious lightweight as *The*

Taming of the Shrew? The answer is two-fold. First, we have thought that one essential of the programme was contrast; that in a programme which included *Measure for Measure* and *Oedipus Rex*, the third play should be less inclined to stir the emotions than to tickle the ribs. Second, and even more practical, the box-office success of a theatrical undertaking depends less upon the choice of play than upon that of the leading actor. This may not be a Good Thing, but in my opinion it is a fact. A Star Name not merely attracts customers to see this particular actor, but it is a kind of guarantee that the whole enterprise is likely to be of good standard. So far Stratford has been fortunate in getting two leading actors of this extremely limited top class, but the programme has had to be chosen to suit their personalities and inclinations. This is quite as it should be. It would be unwise to announce the production of, for instance, *King Lear*—a play which we have been urged to do—unless we first knew that we could command the services of an actor whom we thought attractive to the public, suitable to the part, and who was eager to play it.

Since the inception of the Festival, those responsible for its programme have been under quite a barrage of requests for the 'better known' plays of Shakespeare. I am not quite sure what this means. Perhaps it means the plays which are most often produced. *Hamlet* is the play which has been the most often produced and, surprisingly, *Romeo and Juliet* comes next. Hamlet too, as a character, has been the subject of more books, not merely than any other character in Shakespeare, or indeed in any other author; he has been the subject of more books in English than anyone who ever lived, with just two exceptions: Napoleon Bonaparte and Jesus Christ. Perhaps the 'better known' plays are

163

those which are fullest of the kind of quotations which find their way into the propaganda of insurance companies and car manufacturers, and which Ethel reproduces in chain-stitch and Aubrey in pokerwork. *Hamlet,* again is easily first in this category ('For thine especial safety') ; *As You Like It* ('seven ages') and *The Merchant of Venice* ('quality of mercy') are runners-up. Or perhaps the 'better known' plays are those which appear most often in the Exam Syllabus, and consequently are most vigorously pumped into the young. Though I do not know which these are in Canada, I am in a position to know what they are in Britain: *Macbeth, Julius Caesar, Twelfth Night, Midsummer Night's Dream, The Merchant of Venice, As You Like It,* and *Henry the Fifth.* I cannot for the life of me find any reason for the choice of this particular group. All seven are great works of art; none of them, in my view, is a bit suitable for study in class by people under sixteen. But, granted that they may be, why is *Macbeth,* for instance, preferred to *Hamlet,* or *Julius Caesar* to *Coriolanus?* But there it is. These seem to be considered the most suitable for schools, and therefore are possibly the 'best known' of Shakespeare's plays.

While the choice of programme must continue to be governed by the exigencies of casting, I should have thought that to show some of the less familiar plays, the ones that scarcely ever get a professional showing, was one of the valuable functions of a Festival. The unfamiliarity of these plays must by no means be taken to imply that their quality is inferior.

The Festival has also been given quite a number of lectures on the moral standards of the plays chosen. *Measure for Measure* and *All's Well* were both faulted for not being 'pleasant'. Granted that everyone has a right to his own opinions, artistic or moral, I suggest that to expect Shakespeare to be a moral propagandist is entirely to mistake the man. The greatest critics, though they are wildly at odds on many matters, speak with one voice on this point: they agree that Shakespeare's pre-eminence is due to the miraculous understanding he shows of human nature. He is concerned to interpret his characters but not to draw moral conclusions about them. Moral judgments imply bias, incompatible with the impartiality, the all-embracing sympathy which gives to Shakespeare his godlike stature.

There is not a single one of Shakespeare's plays which is entirely 'nice', or which is not calculated to put 'ideas' into the heads of impressionable people. Those who are afraid to admit the nastiness latent in every human creature had better stay away from Shakespeare. I guess they are fully entitled to wage war on what they regard as evil, but I sincerely trust that they never succeed in establishing the sort of moral censorship which existed in Victorian England. We laugh nowadays at Dr. Bowdler, but it is still all too possible for otherwise rational people to allow themselves to be worked into a high state of moral indignation over the supposed impropriety of what conflicts with their own standards not of moral but merely of conventional behaviour. Mad results follow, a sort of moral McCarthyism, the most illiberal and vicious thinking and action in the name of purity and virtue.

A CLASSICAL POLICY is open to the objection that it makes no provision for the production of new plays. And I have heard it argued that a Festival which offers

165

no encouragement to Canadian authors has no right to consider itself a Canadian institution.

This argument does not seem to me to be sound. It is true that, if the policy at Stratford is only to do classical plays, then the Canadian dramatist does not receive the direct encouragement of performance and royalties. But he does stand to gain in several indirect but important ways. First, it will do his plays **no harm** if, when they do get performed, there are players at hand who have received the more various and far-reaching experience which only a classical programme can provide. Secondly, it will do his plays no harm if they meet an audience whose imaginative range and critical capacity have been extended by some first-hand acquaintance with classical performance. Thirdly— and this I suggest with humility because I know very few of the Canadian plays—I cannot conceive but that a Festival of Classics done in Canada will be a useful exemplar to contemporary Canadian dramatists. Any dramatist of quality, no matter how revolutionary, how 'original', his work may be, can learn valuably from the classics of dramatic literature. And he can learn only so much from reading. It is as important for him to see performances of the Classics as it is for him to see performances of the work of his contemporaries. I cannot therefore agree that a Festival of Drama at which only classical plays are given would have nothing to offer to Canadian dramatists.

Possibly a Festival's claim to be a Canadian institution might be based upon the fact that the company of actors was overwhelmingly Canadian. I don't know. I don't know how far it may be possible to interpret a classical play in a distinctively Canadian way. I am not even quite sure that there is a distinctively Canadian way of doing anything. I am not even sure, despite

166

innumerable legends in support of the idea, that there is a distinctively British, French, Jewish or Chinese way of doing anything. And perhaps Canada—apart from French-Canada—has not been settled long enough for distinctive habits of thought, feeling and expression to have grown out of the effects its climate and its soil have had on the inhabitants. Anyway it is hardly conceivable that an environment so vast and various as the Dominion of Canada could ever, even a hundred years ago in the period when the ideas of Nationality and Nationalism were most flourishing, have produced a single distinctive national type. And surely it is even less likely to be produced now, when, under the pressure of modern industrial development, all geographical and ethnological differences are being ironed out, and when the whole tendency of the age is towards greater and greater standardization.

Nevertheless it is desirable that Canadians should try to assimilate classical works of art as part of their own heritage, not just regard them as imports, acquired at second-hand from overseas. And I think that this assimilation is one of the things that the Stratford Festival ought to be most concerned to assist.

Shakespeare is in one sense a local Warwickshire dramatist. A great part of his magic derives from the wonderful, and often wonderfully inappropriate way he uses his own youthful environment as the basis of his imaginary world. The wood near Athens, for instance, where Lysander, Demetrius, Hermia and Helena have their adventures, does not attempt to suggest the rocks and olive trees near the real city of Athens; but evokes rather the image of the beech and oak woods of Warwickshire. The house where Olivia lives in *Twelfth Night*, with its chantry, its orchard, its buttery hatch, is a Warwickshire manor house, far, far

167

removed from anything which might be expected in a realistic Illyria. But Shakespeare is, of course, far more than a local dramatist. His ideas have a universality and a truth to common human experience which far transcends geographical boundaries. Northumberland, for instance, is, in dialect, landscape and occupation, just as different from Warwickshire as is Western Ontario. Can there, therefore, be any good reason why, with the common bond of the British language, Shakespeare should not seem as indigenous to Western Ontario as he does to Northumberland?

The process of assimilation will be easier if a style of performance can be found which does not emphasize the English-ness so much as the universality of Shakespeare's work. This will be easier still if the universality can be clearly related to current ways of speaking and behaving.

Naturally this does not imply that all the plays should be given in the speech and manner of that myth, the Common Man. That would just be an absurd style for Shakespearean performance. The great personages of Shakespeare can no more be reduced to the level of the Common Man in Canada than they can be in England. In *Coriolanus*, for instance, the whole play is based on the utter contempt of the chief character for the Common Man. The whole point of Great Personages is their difference in character from the Common Man, whom they resemble only in species. In England a good performance of Shakespeare is a presentation of characters who, while in no way reduced in stature, are still recognizable as people like ourselves, still part of the current scene. So it could and should be in Canada.

Some of the plays are more easily related to contemporary manners than others. *Henry VIII*, for instance, is concerned with a particular historical context and has only a remote connection with any other environment or group of people. Inevitably this is so with all the historical chronicles. But many of the tragedies and romances are amazingly independent of details of period or environment, and are consequently more adaptable to transplantation.

Our production at Stratford of *All's Well* made no attempt at setting the play in any realistic or identifiable time or place, but it did attempt to relate the people and the story to contemporary life. I think, from the cordiality of its reception and the evident appreciation of its humour, that the artists did establish some correspondence between the characters they played and the sort of people who are familiar to all of us in daily life. And this, I hope and believe, had the effect, not of reducing the play to a commonplace and journalistic level, but rather of suggesting the exciting and romantic possibilities of real life.

Now, while I hope that performances of the Classics at Stratford may seek to have a distinctively Canadian flavour, I trust that this will not give rise to too narrowly and exclusively 'National' a policy. The result of such a policy is formidably exemplified in the Abbey Theatre in Dublin. In its earlier days, under the guidance first of Lady Gregory, then of Yeats, then of Lennox Robinson, there was a continuous attempt to train the company in more various and important material than just Folk Plays. The Folk Plays, however, were always more popular because they were so much better done. The actors, absolutely brilliant in the portrayal of an environment which they knew well and in dialect which was their own, never rose above a rather feebly amateurish level in classical or foreign works. Consequently the Folk Plays began more and

169

more to dominate the repertoire, and the players began
less and less to bother about extending their technical,
imaginative and intellectual range. Then about twenty-
five years ago, in return for a very small subsidy from
the State, the Abbey Theatre agreed to submit to
various political conditions. The chief one was that
any actor, before being allowed to speak English in the
Abbey company, must pass an exam in the Irish
language. The programme now laid even greater stress
than before on the production of new plays by Irish
authors dealing with Irish life. That was reasonable
enough, and inevitable in a period of long-suppressed
ebullient Nationalism. But unfortunately the Free State
saw fit to impose a severe moral censorship, and the
Chairman of the Abbey Board is now neither a literary
nor a theatrical man; he is a politician. The result is
that the quality of the productions has declined to a
level entirely pedestrian and commonplace. Here and
there are good individual performances when a player
of talent is happily cast. But in general the theatre has
lost almost all cultural importance. Where once it was
remarkable throughout the whole world, it is now no
longer a centre even of national interest. There can, in
my view, be no real pull-up in quality until players and
audience are both willing to submit to a course of
training in works more demanding and far-reaching,
and until the policy of the theatre is less narrowly and
provincially national.

While we may agree that it is impossible to define
what is, or is not, distinctively Canadian; and while we
may hope that the Theatre in Canada may not develop
in too isolationist a manner, yet we must remember
that what a creative artist needs almost more than
anything else is an attachment to a particular environment, usually that in which he was brought up as a
child.

Again and again one sees in the work of the greatest artists how their strength is derived from geographical roots. Think what the Warwickshire countryside has done to Shakespeare's poetry, or the Athenian to that of Sophocles. The novels of Hardy or George Eliot are saturated in the atmosphere of their author's environment. Ibsen is inescapably the product of Scandinavia; Chekhov, Turgenev, Tolstoi, Dostoevski are unthinkable except against a background of Russia. Although there are some striking instances to the contrary— T. S. Eliot is one, Henry James another—in general it is his childhood's background, where his most impressionable years were spent, which form the background of a mature artist's work.

Canadian artists, if they are to thrive, must express what the Canadian climate, the Canadian soil and their fellow-Canadians have made of them. It is vital for their health as artists; and it is no less vital for the health of the community that those with artistic talents should contribute to its life, instead of taking the first opportunity to escape to places where their gifts are welcomed, understood, respected and even rewarded with money.

It is not always remembered by practical people that, although writers, painters, musicians and the like often display a maddening incapacity to deal with combine harvesters, or to answer letters, or to save money, yet they are not necessarily on that account to be written off as Long-haired No-Goods. They are the voice in which one epoch speaks to another. What is remembered now of the Medicis except through the works of art which they commissioned? The lyrics of Robert Burns are made of far more enduring material than the girders of the Forth Bridge. Long, long after the Canadian railroads have crumbled to dust and are no more than a garbled legend, or, worse, a file in

171

some antiquary's records, a song or a picture from this epoch will speak for us, whose maker is now neither celebrated nor rich nor valued in any way, because we simply do not recognize the power of survival, the liveliness, of what he is making.

It is important, therefore, that Canadians should be able to express their own environment, not only for the artists themselves, not only for the community now, but for posterity. And I think that something of Canada can be expressed even in terms of classical drama, the roots of which may be far removed in time and place. These works can, I think, be *interpreted* into a Canadian idiom, given a Canadian style.

IN THIS CONNECTION it is possible already to see some difference between the style and method of approach of a Canadian and a British company. The Canadians, so it now seems to me, bring a freshness of imagination to bear. They think of the meaning of a line or a scene, about the sort of people they are playing, more first-handedly than their British counterparts. Their ideas spring more from their own experience, and less from experience derived at second-hand from painting, literature, from other actors, from other people's interpretation of life.

Life in Britain is over-interpreted. There is an immense weight of past tradition, and the present is hardly less fraught, with its vast output of psychology and psychological novels, criticism, philosophy, didactic and lyric poetry and so on, all explaining, advising, warning, commenting, interpreting.

In Canada, on the contrary, life is under-interpreted. There is, of course, the daily press. But rightly it conceives its job to be the issue of information rather than exegesis. Information is limited to what passes for news. It is news, for instance, if some mute, inglorious Milton is run over by a bus. It is emphatically not news, if, while still inglorious, before he has become a Personality, he ceases to be mute and writes a poem which may be as influential as *Paradise Lost*. Comparatively few of the Interpretations of Life available to the Canadian public are concerned with specifically Canadian life. For the most part Canadians read foreign books, see foreign films and foreign magazines. As in all foreign-dominated cultures it is all but impossible to keep a sense of proportion about the home-grown article. There is a perverse tendency either to cry it down: a radio progamme is '*only* C.B.C.'; a statesman is '*just* a boy from Guelph'; or, alternatively and equally irrationally, there is the wildly partisan attitude which hails a mediocre local soprano as though she were Melba, places an entirely so-so novel in the same bracket as *War and Peace*.

As I have observed it, the effect of all this on Canadian actors is that, though fresh in outlook, they are rather tentative in expression. In any British company, among the younger members will be a shadow Olivier, a carbon Gielgud, several tasteful reproductions in halftone of Sybil Thorndike; and these young people, who may not be very talented, will have plenty of technical confidence and assurance; they will have plenty of know-how, if a rather limited amount of know-what. Nevertheless, under a director who knows what's what, they can create an effect of very skilful and professional performance.

By contrast I have found the Canadian players rather shy and reluctant to attempt any form of improvisation. The younger people, lacking any outstanding models on which to base their own unformed person-

173

alities and undeveloped techniques, are more nervous and tentative than they need be; and are all too ready to exchange a gawky, gangling, but extremely winning simplicity for the most obvious and conventional methods of expression—stuff they have seen on the films—under the delusion that this is the Right Way.

It is a fallacy prevalent among people without much experience, or else without much intelligence, that there are Right Ways and Wrong Ways. Certainly in art, and I incline to think in all other departments of human activity, Right and Wrong are purely subjective terms. There are no rules of acting, except the most elementary commonsense principles: that, for example, speech must be audible to the audience, action visible. And I can conceive of circumstances where even these need not necessarily apply.

In my view the basic difference between Canadian and British actors amounts to no more than this: the British actors perform, in the 'straight' Theatre at all events, to a public that is sated with professional entertainment, which is bored with mere merit and sighs only for novelty; they are 'noticed' by critics of whom those who are anything more than gossip-writers have long lost any enthusiasm they may once have felt about the Theatre; they are surrounded by expert colleagues of whom there are ten to every one available job. The British actors, in short, experience the advantages and disadvantages of working in a crowded commercial market. In Canada the Theatre is hardly a market at all, has hardly begun to exist. This difference in conditions, however, simple as it is, accounts for a significant difference in style and approach. But this in itself does not substantiate the existence of a distinctively Canadian style.

POTENTIALLY the most distinctive characteristic of Canadian actors is their speech. It is in the speaking that a distinctive national style may, or may not, emerge. And it is here that the policy of the Stratford Festival may possibly have its most interesting results.

It is my view that the plays of Shakespeare should be presented by Canadian actors speaking in a recognizably Canadian manner, rather than speaking in an English which may be supposed, upon rather dubious evidence, to be the English which Shakespeare 'heard'; or in an English such as is currently fashionable in the West End of London; or even in the *macédoine* of dialects which passes for English on the rare occasions when Shakespeare is heard on Broadway.

The problem I believe is this: in England there seems to be some general agreement—far from precise —as to what is considered good and bad speech. There does exist, whether one agrees with the underlying reasons or not, a definable standard of good pronunciation by which one may judge the quality of the speaking in, for instance, a classical play. In Canada, as far as I have been able to discover, there is absolutely no agreement on this point.

In England good speaking is principally distinguished from bad by subtleties of pronunciation, which are quite impossible to reproduce in writing, but which enable a skilled listener to 'place' a speaker in respect of origin, social standing, occupation and so on, with a quite devastating accuracy. Professor Higgins in Shaw's *Pygmalion* is an example of this skill only slightly exaggerated to point the comedy. Certain vowel sounds are notoriously distinguishing in the matter of class: by the way a man says 'Captain Lowndes has thousands and thousands of brown hounds' it is possible to know for an absolute certainty whether or no his grandmother was presented at Court.

Until a very short time ago, 'good' and 'bad' English pronunciation has been a matter of quite arbitrary fashion, conformity or non-conformity with which denoted 'class'. Fashions, naturally, keep changing. It is now permissible to refer to a young female as a 'gurl'; in my youth it was *de rigeur* to say 'gairl'. Seventy years ago it was hopelessly common to say 'isn't it'; one said 'is not it', or, colloquially, 'ain't it' or even 'ain' it'. Now 'isn't it' is acceptable, 'ain't it' is distinguishingly vulgar.

But now the whole question of class-distinction has been inextricably confused by the economic and social upheavals of the past four decades. To be rich is now almost a certain indication that one is vulgar and probably dishonestly evading income tax. Eton and Oxford, once symbols of wealth and privilege, are now more than half occupied by Scholarship Boys, of whom the majority come from Working Class Homes. But that only means that these boys are accustomed to better meals and have pocket money. The Little Lords from the Moated Grange have no pocket money and eat only after Daddy has sold another Gainsborough.

All this will gradually have surprising repercussions on the speaking of the language. But as yet England has not decided what group in the community constitutes the new aristocracy, is not sure who sets the fashions. So, as yet, the old ideas are still dominant, the old standard still prevails; it is still right to 'talk genteel'. In England it is still believed that certain dialects are 'beautiful', notably those spoken in Wales, Cornwall, the South of Ireland and the Highlands of Scotland, which are Celtic in origin, and therefore seem untouched by the vulgarities of unfashionable English. Lowland Scots is quaint but respectable. Yorkshire and Lancashire dialects are the lingo of

176

comedians, of Perfect Screams. In every big city the Middle Classes loathe and despise the way the language is spoken in the slums of their own city. The Middle Classes everywhere seem united about one aspect of speech: English as spoken in Australia is THE END.

This fact, if no other, lets the cat out of the bag. English as spoken in Australia is certainly not very like what passes for upper-class English. It is, according to current fashion in England, thoroughly 'common'. But is it on that account to be considered bad? I think the terms 'good' and 'bad' should apply to speech for some more valid reason. Surely good speech should mean that it is expressive, interesting, intelligible, rather than merely pronounced in the manner that is fashionable in a certain section of English society at a given moment. I consider that I have heard in Australia speech which was quite as expressive and interesting as in London, and voices which, on the whole, were much better produced. It may be the Australian climate—no one can say for sure—but it is significant that Australia, in proportion to her population, has produced so many of the world's best singers. The Opera Houses in London are crawling with Australians; and it is the oddest paradox if they sing well but really do speak badly.

Now back to Canada: is there any clear differentiation of accent and idiom between one locality and another? I have heard it claimed by one intelligent and well-informed person that Canadian speech differed from American as chalk from cheese; and by another that Canadian and American speech resembled each other as pea does pea. Since there is some obvious and considerable variety of American accent, neither of these two persons seemed to be talking sense.

I have myself been quite unable to trace any class distinction in Canadian speech. Of course I am aware that there is a polite conspiracy to pretend that there is no class distinction. But in fact one has only to be in Canada for three days to see that there quite evidently is. No doubt it is easier to move from one income group or one occupation to another in Canada than it is, for example, in Scotland. But it is very questionable whether this is the result of anything more than the fact that in Canada it is much easier at present to get rich quickly, and that in a 'new' country inevitably roots are shallower, habits are less fixed, one moves more readily from place to place, job to job and group to group. But even in Canada it is demonstrably more congenial for like to mix with like. I can only testify that the ugliest, most raucous and unattractive speaking I have heard in Canada has come from the lips, not of roughnecked, horny-handed sons of toil, but from nicely-come-home, expensively educated, sophisticated ladies in Westmount and Rosedale. It was speech, which, as an expert, I would declare to be thoroughly bad in every important respect. Nevertheless it was perfectly acceptable in a Society which was evidently exclusive.

It is probable that, though it is not apparent to the visitor, English as spoken in Canada has begun to develop its own standards of good and bad. But these are not yet so fixed that they cannot be decisively influenced. Stratford could, and possibly may, be quite an important influence in this respect. In the modern world actors probably have more influence upon speech than any other group in the community. They are now widely heard on films, radio and television.

178

Standards of speech adopted at Stratford may quite possibly influence the standard of speech in other theatrical groups, and may thus be widely influential. Since I shall be, for one more year at least, responsible for the pronunciation at Stratford, I shall say what I consider good speech, and why.

The first essential is clarity and audibility. That is largely a matter of clear thinking and an uninhibited wish to communicate. But a speaker may be intelligent and willing and still, for technical reasons, his speech may be confused and hard to hear. For clarity and audibility he will need good voice-production and clear diction: a breath-stream so directed as to produce resonant vowels, these vowel-sounds punctuated by adequately decisive consonants.

But this alone is not enough. An audible sound is not therefore intelligible. Intelligibility is largely a matter of rhythm, stress and phrasing. Phrasing implies the grouping of words; it is, as it were, a subdivision of rhythm, and is vitally important to making clear the logical arrangement of words. For instance, the following is clearly phrased:

> I-love-little-Pussy
> Her-coat-is-so-warm.

It would be possible, though daft, to phrase the words as follows:

> I-love-little
> Pussy-her-coat-is-so-warm.

Technically, phrasing is largely a matter of breath-control, of not breathing except when a pause is really desirable.

Most actors, when speaking what they have learned by heart, break up the speech into very short phrases. They breathe between each phrase, not to give added point to what they are saying, but to give themselves time—and energy—to think what comes next. It is true that a great deal of conversation is conducted in very short phrases:

A. Hiya!
B. Hi!
A. Fine weather.
B. Very fine.
A. Cold, though.
B. Yeah, but fine.
  (Pause)
A. How's Uncle?
B. Fine, thanks.
A. And Auntie?
B. She's just fine too.
A. Good.
  (Pause)
A. Well ... (pause) ... be seeing you.
B. Yeah.
A. 'Bye.
B. 'Bye.

The above dialogue would not be any more taxing to the breath-control than it is to the intellect.

A great deal of conversation, however, also takes place in hugely long phrases, sentence being joined to sentence, topic to topic, without the slightest break or pause of any kind. Most actors have been taught reading, though not all are able to read very well. One of the lessons we were all taught in reading is concerned with phrasing. It is this: a period, or full stop, implies just what its name implies. A comma implies a short pause; a semicolon a slightly longer pause. But in modern usage these punctuation marks imply grammatical rather than rhythmical divisions. Now, in speaking as opposed to reading, the grammar is inclined to take care of itself. One may write: 'I like

180

strawberries comma because they taste so nice.' But in speech the sentence is apt to be more intelligible, as well as lighter on the wing, if the comma is ignored.

The following paragraph is, I hope, correctly punctuated, and would be almost impossible to read if there were no punctuation. But if you imagine it spoken, and spoken in a high state of excitement, it would be natural if all the punctuation marks were ignored and the speech given as one long unbroken phrase:

> There's a man in the room downstairs. He says he's come to mend the boiler; but, my goodness, that's a lie! I mean, he's wearing a mask. Yes, he's got a black scarf sort of thing round his face. Well, I mean, a person would never wear a thing like that just to mend a boiler. That man's a thief, that's what. He's come to open the safe, so he has. He's come to steal the Rajah's Emerald.

To speak this all in one phrase requires rather good breath-control. It would be utterly impossible to do so, unless the speech were known extremely fluently. Every ounce of energy is required for the delivery of the speech, none can be spared to refresh the cells of the brain or wherever the seat of memory may be. Therefore any actor who has not got the speech absolutely pat, at his fingers' ends, as the saying goes, will require to breathe at least once, probably twice, during its course. Any inexperienced speaker will instinctively pause at the full stops. But it is my opinion that the speech delivered with pauses remains intelligible, but is very much less expressive than when delivered at headlong speed, and with no pauses whatsoever. In a play it is essential to seek for the most expressive way of delivering a speech; and it is often necessary to choose the faster of two equally expressive alternatives.

Shakespeare is full of passages whose mere intelligibility depends upon a long phrase, upon ignoring punctuation and offering to the audience the meaning of a whole chunk, rather than the separate meanings of a number of clauses. Here is an instance; Macbeth speaks to the Murderers:

> Ay, in the catalogue ye go for men;
> As hounds and greyhounds, mongrels, spaniels, curs,
> Shoughs, water-rugs, and demi-wolves, are clept
> All by the name of dogs: the valued file
> Distinguishes the swift, the slow, the subtle,   5
> The housekeeper, the hunter, every one
> According to the gift which bounteous nature
> Hath in him closed; whereby he does receive
> Particular addition, from the bill
> That writes them all alike: and so of men.   10
> Now, if you have a station in the file,
> Not i' th' worst rank of manhood, say't
> And I will put that business in your bosoms,
> Whose execution takes your enemy off;
> Grapples you to the heart and love of us,   15
> Who wear our health but sickly in his life,
> Which in his death were perfect.

I suggest that the first break cannot occur till the middle of line 4, after the word 'dogs'. I do not think it is right to breathe again till the middle of line 10, after 'alike'. Thereafter the pausing becomes less a matter of sense than of taste. I would pause again briefly at the end of line 10, after 'and so of men', so that this phrase is isolated between short pauses. Then I would certainly go straight on to the end of line 15, 'love of us', and, if possible, would even go to the end of the speech, greatly slowing down the speed, however, and increasing the emphasis in the important last two lines, stressing the double antithesis of 'sickly-perfect life-death'. Remember that this speech is tentative, careful, rather than excited. It would be inappropriate to speak rapidly. The demand on breath-control is the greater therefore.

In general a good speaker should be able to speak, loudly and at moderate speed, seven lines of blank verse without a breath. But almost all actors, unless forced by a director or by the ineluctable sense of their lines, will breathe far oftener. An inexperienced person will want to breathe at least twice in every three lines. Meaningless pauses and breaks in the sense, due to inadequate breath-control, are in my opinion the single worst fault in contemporary acting.

A speech must not only be phrased, it must also be inflected; that is to say, as well as rhythm it must have a tune. Inflection is the steering of the voice up and down in pitch. English as spoken in America and Canada is a much less sharply inflected language than as spoken in the British Isles. In Britain the tunes in which we speak have a much wider compass. As a kind of compensation for lack of inflection, American dialects have developed great subtlety and variety of rhythm. In acting, this is valuable in comedy; the dry, wisecracking type of humour can be very happily expressed in American. But in declamation it is essential for an actor to use the full compass of his voice. Most people ought to have about two octaves at command. For the building up of a big rhetorical climax an actor must have his entire voice in good working order from top to bottom. Most voices are in reasonable trim as regards the middle register, where we habitually speak, but the top and bottom are apt to be rusty from lack of use. Most people's voices are hoarse and growly and feeble at the bottom, and at the top pinched and shrill.

In the matter of inflection most of us incline to monotony, shy people being unable to inflect a sentence, except in the feeblest, most tentative way. It is essential for an actor to develop a good ear for inflection and to avoid the monotonous and conventional tunes which most of us habitually use.

Of all the speakers whom I have heard, Sir John Gielgud makes the best use of inflection. Indeed I think that in respect of rhetoric he is the best of contemporary actors in the English language. The voice is a good one, though not outstanding; it is not entirely well produced, being pinched and thin at the top; it is the innate musicality of rhythm, stress and melody, combined with a crystal clarity of intention, which makes his speech so faithful an interpreter of a witty mind and a sensitive heart.

One more aspect of voice production must be mentioned: colour. Vocal colour is hard to define except by audible example. It is produced by directing the breath stream so as to produce more, or less, nasal resonance. In general, 'bright' colour indicates the sort of tone which is produced by plenty of nasal resonance and a powerful breath stream, the sort of tone appropriate to a shout of triumph or joy; a tone analogous to that of a trumpet. 'Dark' tone indicates the kind of sound produced by using very little nasal resonance, by allowing the resonance to emanate almost entirely from the throat and chest, and by using a large amount of breath for a comparatively small tone. This produces the sort of sound associated with awe, fear, low sinister threats and that sort of thing.

I have merely tried to explain the meaning of the term 'tone-colour' by giving two very broad, obvious instances. The whole point, however, is that the ear is so acutely and subtly sensitive to shades of vocal colour that we can detect in a moment, and with extraordinary precision, what is a speaker's mood, simply by listening to his tone. One can, for instance, gauge the exact degree of cordiality in a farewell, or perceive a controlled asperity, a degree of condescension or of servility, in the merest commonplace.

So exquisitely adjusted is the speech mechanism of each of us, that, without knowing it, we are all the time performing small prodigies of breath control, voice production, changes of rhythm and colour. Listen on the telephone and note how subtle are the pauses, how delicate the indications by stress, rhythm, colour, inflection and volume, which enable one to deduce that one's interlocutor is telling a lie. Then reflect how exquisitely adjusted is the mechanism first of hearing, then of deduction, which enables one to be so certain.

A well-equipped actor must be in conscious control of all this vocal and aural mechanism, which by most of us is simply used instinctively.

FINALLY WE COME to the matter of pronunciation. As I have said above, I think it would be quite wrong for Canadian actors to try to pronounce the words of a classical play in an assumed 'English' accent. It really seems of no importance whether the word 'No' is pronounced in what passes in London for good English, or with the very much more nasal production which is usual in Canada, and which makes the word sound to British ears like 'Naw'. It could not matter less. There should, however, be some uniformity, some agreement as to how nasal it is permissible to be. Such agreement will eventually emerge; I think it is emerging already; most of the Canadian actors who are seriously interested in their craft, as opposed to their careers, have already at command what seems to me an entirely acceptable accent. No one could mistake them for Englishmen, yet they avoid the more rasping mannerisms and slovenliness of much current Canadian speech.

As a director I would not dream of telling an actor how to pronounce his words, except where rhythmic

185

stress demands a change from what he is doing, or where there is some need to unify the pronunciation of the same word by two actors, each of whom may be pronouncing it differently and each of whose pronunciations may be justifiable (e.g. 'in*dec*orous' or 'inde*cor*ous'; 'neether' or 'nyether'), or where his pronunciation seems to belie his characterization.

For instance I would check an actor who was cast to play the role of an educated person, if he used the exaggerated and typically Canadian final '—er' (e.g. 'Mother' pronounced 'Mawthurr'), if he allowed this 'r' sound to distort the precedent vowel ('sturrt the curr' for 'start the car'). Of course, I admit the rightness of sounding the 'r' in these words. 'Staht the cah' is as vulgar in England as it is laughable in Canada. I would check him if he slurred his dental consonants *à l'américaine* ('wazza maddurr' for 'what's the matter'); if he swallowed his 'l' sounds *à l'écossaise*; if he slurred his vowel sounds so as to make a monosyllable out of a dissyllabic word ('c'rect' or even 'c'reck' for 'correct'), if he made a dissyllabic out of a trisyllabic word ('Tranna' for 'Toronto' or 'Can'da' for 'Canada'). I am aware that these 'mistakes' and many others —my list does not pretend to be exhaustive, merely indicative—are made by many Canadians of the very highest education and most eminent attainments. They still seem to me, on principle, to be 'bad' speaking, because slurring of syllables interferes with the rhythm and meaning of words; slurring of consonants deprives language of variety and vitality; the typical Canadian emphasis on '—er' gives disproportionate weight to this sound in relation to others, leads to distortion of vowel sounds and is the cause, in my opinion, of a great deal of injurious voice production induced by tightening throat and jaw muscles on this syllable. I am trying,

186

in fact, to maintain that I object to these mannerisms, not because they infringe British class tabus, and British standards of pronunciation based on fashion, but because their use makes a speaker less expressive.

FINALLY TO RETURN to practical matters of policy at Stratford, it is my view that for several more years it will be necessary, for business reasons, to import 'stars', if suitable stars are available. This is not because I think that they act better than the best of the Canadians. It is a matter of *réclame*. Because there has hitherto been so little opportunity for actors in Canada, none of the Canadian men and women have yet been able to make, in Canada, the sort of reputation which sells literally thousands of tickets in advance. To a project on the scale of Stratford such an advance sale is an absolute necessity.

It is a melancholy fact that reputations of the required magnitude are no longer made in the Theatre. It takes the film industry to create them, with its enormous distribution and consequently enormous resources available for publicity. But to be a film star it is not always necessary to be a well equipped or even a talented actor. It is enough to have those qualities of appearance which make the fans want to gobble you up.

In the ranks of the film stars there are very, very few people who could begin to make a showing in any of the great classical roles, and of those few there are not many who care to take the risk of trying. It is not easy to get within miles of the bull's-eye in *Lear, Othello, Macbeth* or any of the great Shakespearean spouting whales. It is all too easy to come a highly conspicuous cropper. None of the careerists will take

187

this kind of risk. Only a sincere artist will dare it; and even so he will only be prepared to do so under direction and in an ensemble which inspires his confidence, and in a role of his own choice.

It can therefore be seen how very much easier it would be to choose the programme or to make long term plans for a Festival, if the Festival could be independent of the services of this small group of actors before whose feet, incidentally, every management in the English-speaking world is simultaneously laying its jewels—many of them enormously more glittering than the modest chaplet which Stratford can bestow.

Meantime it is our policy to 'build up' those of the Canadian artists who seem to us to have most promise —and in this matter judgment must always be subjective and often wrong—by giving them the best opportunities and the best publicity which we can afford. Already Canadian artists, whose reputation outside Canada was not widely known, have played leading parts in the Festival and have been given prominent place in the advertisements. There is, of course, a possibility that Canadians, who make a brilliant showing at Stratford or elsewhere in Canada, will be bought up by foreign interests. But this is highly desirable, both in the interests of the artists themselves and of the whole health of the Theatre in Canada. It is a good thing when Mr. A or Miss B are picked out and given some conspicuous opportunity in New York or Hollywood or London. It is then up to Canada to create such a Theatre at home that Mr. A and Miss B will be glad and proud to return, bringing their sheaves with them.

Eventually no doubt it will be possible for Stratford to put on an all-Canadian cast. But this, in my opinion, is not necessarily a desirable aim. I hope rather that

188

the Governors will adopt a policy which will allow some interchange between Canada and the Theatre in other parts of the English-speaking world. In my opinion it is essential that this should be a two-way traffic. Already, under the banner of Stratford, this export/import has begun. A limited number of British artists have taken part in the Festival, and a fund has been started whereby young Canadian artists can go to Britain for a period of study and training and a general broadening of horizon. Eventually, I hope, this scheme may enable the Canadian artists to travel, not as students, but as members of the professional Theatre abroad.

So much for the acting side. Hitherto it has been found necessary to import heads of the staffs who make the clothes, properties, armour and so on. These positions will be held by Canadians when, and if, the live Theatre in Canada develops enough impetus to enable suitable people to earn a year-round livelihood in Canada at no lower wages, with no worse prospects, and doing no less interesting work than they would get elsewhere. Meantime under experienced imported leadership there is valuable training available for young men and women who wish to learn, and be paid while learning, the various crafts ancillary to the production of a play.

Eventually there must be a Canadian director, but I do not think such an appointment can be made as yet. There are no opportunities at present in Canada for a director to get the necessary experience of large-scale production, or the reputation necessary to attract eminent artists to work with him. By degrees these opportunities will begin to be available; and gradually, if the Festival becomes an annual affair, Stratford will be able to give opportunities for young directors to get their foot in the door, not necessarily by entrusting them with the responsibility for the main productions, but by putting them in charge of understudies' rehearsals, special performances and so on.

As YET, it has only been possible to plan each Festival separately and to look no further ahead than the next year. Now that it begins to be not only possible but necessary to take a longer view, I have endeavoured to suggest here what I am thinking and feeling—now. I sincerely hope that I have not given an impression of being dogmatic, or too set in my views. In the Theatre, as in, I suppose, all other activities, one has to find some middle way between principle and expediency. Principles are the necessary stars to steer by; but it is no good taking such a rigid attitude that one refuses to abandon course for a moment in order to avoid coming to grief on the rocks of particular circumstance. And the Theatre is such a speculative, uppy-downy kind of business that long-term plans can never be made with the confidence that is possible in business of a more stable character. The most carefully formulated theatrical plans are always contingent upon the co-operation of a group of *people*. Personalities and personal relations are all-important.

Artists can be put under contract, signed and sealed with seven seals, or seventy times seven. Such documents can compel the formalities of service to be rendered. They are powerless to compel the enthusiastic, congenial co-operation which alone produces any valuable result in the Theatre. A bereavement, a quarrel, a slip on the stairs, laryngitis, hiccoughs—and a plan which has taken months to prepare, in which hundreds of thousands of dollars have been invested, crashes to the ground in useless fragments.

Not only is the Theatre in general a chancy and unpredictable business; he would be indeed a rash man who made too many generalizations about its future in Canada. We none of us quite know what television may yet mean to the Theatre. We none of us know whether, at any moment, the Canadian Theatre may not be made a conspicuous but absolutely impotent pawn in the great, sprawling, cynically impersonal chess-game, which is being played between Capital and Labour on the American continent. We none of us know whether, at any moment, our whole civilization may not be staked on the even more sprawling chess-game which is being played by two even vaguer, more fantastically and irrationally abstract contestants, labelled East and West.

But there it is. If life is to go on, then action must take place; action must be based on some kind of plan; plans must be based on some kind of aspiration; aspiration on some kind of faith. I have tried to state an outline of what seems to me reasonable plans for Stratford's future. Let me conclude by a very brief confession of the faith on which they are based.

I believe that a Theatre, where live actors perform plays to an audience which is there in the flesh before them, will survive all threats from powerfully organized industries, which pump prefabricated drama out of cans and blowers and contraptions of one kind and another. The struggle for survival may often be severe and will often batter the old Theatre about severely. Indeed from time to time it may be hardly recognizable; but it will survive. It will survive as long as mankind demands to be amused, terrified, instructed, shocked, corrupted and uplifted by tales told in the manner which will always remain mankind's most vivid and powerful manner of communication. I believe that the purpose of the Theatre is to show man-

191

I believe that this purpose is ill served by *consciously* endeavouring to use the Theatre as a moral, social or political 'influence'. It cannot avoid being all three. Its ministers must not be so arrogant as to believe their work is to Do Good to their fellow-men. Their work is to glorify their Creator by expressing themselves. They will choose the material to express themselves which they feel, more than think, will suit what they believe they have it in them, from time to time, to express. In this choice they will feel 'guided' or 'inspired', as all God's prophets have been, from Elijah down to the humblest, dottiest, squalidest persons who have believed themselves to be guided and inspired. If this is not so, then for me the term Artist is entirely meaningless.

I believe that the Theatre makes its effect not by means of illusion, but by Ritual.

People do not believe that what they see and hear in the theatre is 'really' happening. Action on the stage is a stylized re-enactment of real action, which is then imagined by the audience. The re-enactment is not merely an imitation but a symbol of the real thing. If I may quote this instance without irreverence, it expresses the point clearly: the priest in Holy Communion re-enacts with imitative but symbolic gestures the breaking of bread and pouring of wine. He is at that moment an actor impersonating Christ in a very solemn drama. The congregation or audience, is under no illusion that at that moment he really *is* Christ. It should however have participated in the ritual with sufficient fervour to be rapt, literally 'taken out of itself', to the extent that it shares the emotion which the priest or actor is suggesting—it completes the cycle of action and reaction, its function is not passive but active. This, I think, is exactly what happens to an audience at a successful theatrical performance.

Just as the sacred drama of Holy Communion is

non-illusionary, so is the sacred drama of *Oedipus Rex*, where the actor (also originally a priest) impersonates a symbol of sacrifice. Equally non-illusionary though more secular is *Macbeth*, for instance, where the protagonist performs actions symbolical of Regicide, Usurpation, Remorse and so on. The same principle can, in my view, be applied to all drama; and in all drama, even the most frivolous, I think that there is some attempt to relate the participants to God, or at least to some aspect of God, albeit such aspects are often those represented in Greece by such figures as Dionysus, Apollo and Aphrodite.

The Theatre is the direct descendant of Fertility Rites, War Dances, and all the corporate ritual expressions by means of which our primitive ancestors, often wiser than their progeny, sought to relate themselves to God, or the gods, the great abstract forces, which cannot be apprehended by reason; but in whose existence reason compels us to believe.

Reason alone is not enough. Faith alone is not enough, though it can move a mountain. Faith allied to reason can move a mountain for a reasonable purpose.

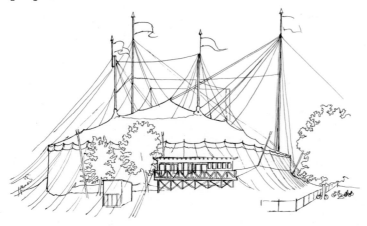

The Tent from the River side showing the Green Room